To Err is Woman

OBIORA OJI

authorHOUSE

AuthorHouse™
1663 Liberty Drive
Bloomington, IN 47403
www.authorhouse.com
Phone: 833-262-8899

© 2020 Obiora Oji. All rights reserved.

No part of this book may be reproduced, stored in a retrieval system, or transmitted by any means without the written permission of the author.

Published by AuthorHouse 11/04/2020

ISBN: 978-1-6655-0558-1 (sc)
ISBN: 978-1-6655-0556-7 (hc)
ISBN: 978-1-6655-0557-4 (e)

Library of Congress Control Number: 2020921064

Print information available on the last page.

Any people depicted in stock imagery provided by Getty Images are models, and such images are being used for illustrative purposes only.
Certain stock imagery © Getty Images.

This book is printed on acid-free paper.

Because of the dynamic nature of the Internet, any web addresses or links contained in this book may have changed since publication and may no longer be valid. The views expressed in this work are solely those of the author and do not necessarily reflect the views of the publisher, and the publisher hereby disclaims any responsibility for them.

To Asterisk, the daughter I haven't had.

1

For another moment, Stephen's eyes strayed to the clock at the tail of the kitchen. He had to stretch his ciliary muscles to make out precisely what time it read. It was rather too obvious that the clock was as oddly placed as it was too small for the long hall that was his kitchen. 5.42p.m.

Approximately fifty five minutes had slipped by since he set out on this voluntary task. He twitched his nostrils hoping to catch the faintest fragrance from his efforts: Nothing.

Just then, ugly reminisces of his first ever experience as a cook crept into his mind. They always made him shudder and they resurged- even when he entered the kitchen to do something as trivial as fetching cutleries. Thankfully, he rarely came this way..but even now, he was starting to doubt whether he could pull this off successfully.

Stephen was barely ten years old then and his mother had asked him to peel some potatoes for dinner while she rushed to attend to an emergency summon at the village market square- Ekiano. It was late Friday evening and with a little common sense, he knew it was going to be fried potatoes and maybe *akamu* for dinner. There was no *akamu* in the house but he reasoned that the Mum would eventually get it on her way back from Ekiano. Driven by a passion to impress- a trait he hadn't lost even till hither days- the little boy had proceeded to make the dinner all by himself.

Like tonight, his only intention was to pull off a pleasant surprise. But that was not to be. Stephen shuddered again.

In the order that he remembered or he felt he remembered, he had placed the oil on the fire and then strolled a brief distance away from the hut to pick a couple of fire-sticks. He was certain there would be need for more in the course of the preparations.

Stephen was by no means prepared for what he met on his return. The steaming oil had filled the entire *Uno ekwu* with thick smoke. Just a peep in and he had choked abit. He couldn't possibly understand what it was that had gone wrong but he knew enough to tie up the adage, 'No smoke without fire.' For a ten year old, he was by no means dull. He had darted to the nearest drum, fetched a bucketful and without any further hesitation, he plunged the water at the area where he supposed the fire was coming from.

In response, there was a thunderous explosion. The sound had sent him on the floor, his empty bucket in hand. His eyes welled up- more from frustration. He was lucky that he had attempted the fire-fighting from the edge of the kitchen door.

Excitement gave way to dejection as he sat put on the floor, whimpering and coughing-on repeat until Mama returned about half an hour later.

Stephen had been spanked- his noble intentions not withstanding and forbade from entering the kitchen until he grew older.

He heaved in painful relief. His parents were already long dead but he wasn't sure he had grown older.

The pool of sweat that had gathered across his brows called out to him for the first time.

'Gosh,' he exhaled. He couldn't tell how many *goshes* he had had to say this evening. Memories are a heavy load, he thought to himself as he drew up his *Agbada* and mopped the sweat away. He just hoped these sweats would pay off.

Stephen Avri was 'Made in Scratchland'. His upbringing left a detailed imprint on his perspective of and attitude to life.

To live was to Struggle. That was his surviving principle and only once- in his thirty eight years on earth had he had to doubt that maxim. From birth, life had not really been cruel. He was the single surviving issue of a very diligent marriage, having lost his siblings routinely to some untagged childhood illnesses. He could vividly remember the elaborate coronation-like celebrations that marked his fourth birthday and subconsciously he had began to believe that since he could make it past three, he was billed to live forever. There were tons and tons of priveleges that came with his only status. How he warmed up to them. However the realities of having to lose his father and mother at thirteen and sixteen respectively followed by the greed of dubious Uncles aroused him significantly. At sixteen and even now, he knew he was not born to fill the shoes of a local champion. He didn't have to worry one bit about the stolen lands and other entitlements. Young Avri had just kept pace with his dreams, pushed his way through school and graduated with a First Class Honours in Accountancy- the only in nine preceding sets. The University College swiftly offered him a place for Master's degree free of charge but six months into his study, he got a scholarship space at the University of Birmingham for the same purpose.

He was a man perfect in his timings. At exactly 26, Stephen Avri completed his Masters, in visibly flying colors and braced up for the challenges of the labor market. He was an instant hit. Buffered by streams of recommendations from his lecturers at the Birmingham University, he had started off with the Merchant Insurers Ltd in Leeds- renowned for their thrifty management of shipping firms stocks and trades. Management was inept to Stephen. He wasted no time in unearthing his accounting prowess and the heap of experiences he had gathered back home in Nigeria. In thirty three months, Stephen was General Manager, Customer Service Relations at the firm and had seven scores of employees directly under his supervision. His trademark down to earth listening style and sometimes queer analysis of situations were unprecedented and even till date, he got letters of appreciations from his previous staff. He was a team leader and although he had spent just about eight months on that post, the characters of most his staff were permanently polished.

In five rapid years, Stephen's career span through London, a brief stint in Mexico where he had been retained followed an International Conference on Chartered Accounting.

He had presented a paper in the seminar and his brilliance had shone. The organisers of the meeting had put up a 'hold-back' package to lure him to stay on. It wasn't even the monetary gains that enticed him to remain; his life was dedicated to imparting as much knowledge as he could when given the audience. Half a year later, he was traded between the patent company, Merchant Insurance and Commerzbank in Paris. He was not the type to yet bother about the figures of these transactions. The London firm had been classically fair to him and inspite of the ingenuinity of his fast rising brand, he trusted that his back would ultimately be covered both financially and diplomatically.

Commerzbank was a multinational bank, partly owned by the French, Swiss and British. The scourge of a new language was quickly addressed within two months. They had their own quick fix French tutor and within six weeks, Stephen was flowing like he had been there for two years. It was a system that worked to maximum effectiveness. As always, his reputation had preceded him and there was little or nothing he could do to miss scrutiny but the typical Stephen was too busy investing all of himself in the job that he didn't notice the different shades of green in more than a few eyes nor did he catch any hints from the stiffness that masked particular conversations.

'I think I like you,' she half-whispered as she sat on the edge of his table. 'And I am going to have you.' Stephen didn't have to glance up. He had heard that voice for the most part of his two years stay and even her fragrance was uncomfortably familiar. Nicole had stepped into the Banker's lounge in her usual loud fashion, exchanged hearty greetings with a string of colleagues and even as she glided towards Stephen, she could swear she had his attention in spite of his refusal to look up. It was a mystery she had taken upon herself to solve and even though it had unwittingly turned into an obsession, it bothered her little that it was becoming increasingly clear that she was haunting Stephen Avri.

'Hi. Nicole,' Stephen muttered, shifting his tea cup farther from the edge of her domineering ass. His voice was calm and calculated though his mind was in clusters of confusion. Nicole was not the picture of the lady he dreamed of. She was blonde, French and pretty. She was an engulfing company to have and quite versed in routine flamboyant living. The fact that she was markedly fluent in English made it easier for her to access him and even in those earlier days when Stephen was bulldozing his way through French, she was quick to act Translator for him.

'Do you mind if I joined you.' She had already sat down on the adjacent chair. Stephen shook his head. He knew she cared little whether he minded or not. She was a woman used to having her ways. They had sat through lunch in dismal silence, each pondering on what move would score maximal points. They were coming from very different perspectives. The cat-rat game; the battle line had been clearly drawn by Nicole's introductory remarks and deep within Stephen, he worried a tiny bit. What gave this woman this degree of confidence?

At the end of a quiet session, Stephen had finished his meal first and without a care about courtesy excused himself. As he walked away, he had felt the bore of Nicole's eyes following him out of the hall. Outside the hall, he had straightened his suit and done his typical 'Gosh'.

'You really think it was wisdom to leave me behind?' Stephen was visibly startled. He could swear he had come out unfollowed. How did Nicole make it here in a flash?

'I have work to do,' he started 'it was supposed to be a short break.' Nicole nodded in sheer disbelief.

'Pity me-Miss Idle.' The sarcasm was not lost.

'Am sorry, Nicole but this is neither the right place nor the time for our endless arguments.' He was starting to walk away. 'We will make out a better-'

'You lie Stephen' she was nearly screaming. 'You've been saying that line for ages.'

Stephen nodded and fled. He couldn't allow complications at this stage of his life. He and Nicole had formed some admirable partnership earlier on but he was bent on changing that notion and fast too. He was never going to be tagged alongside Monsieur Pierre's secretary and mistress. Mr Pierre was the Chairman of Commerzbank and although his relationship with Stephen had no inks of that stray fondness, the younger man needed no second warnings to do some rechecks immediately he caught wind of the illicit relationship. But the harder he ran, the more impossible Nicole proved and this turned out to be a huge test of resilience from both parties.

On the November of Stephen's fifth year at Commerzbank, he was nominated alongside three other foreigners for the Expatriate of the Year Award. He was the only one from the big bank and the only non-European in the list. The prize had amongst other things, an automatic slot for French citizenship. There was literally no competition.

They were all notable achievers in their respective fields but as per relevance to the national economy and milestone movers, Stephen outshone all of them. Politics aside, it was hard to imagine a government who would ditch a financial asset for other sector-achievers. Mr. Avri's accolades were a beacon and they were sheer symptoms of the routine life of hardwork, dedication and repetitive success.

The twenty eight of November had been slated for the ceremony cum the announcement of the grand winner and the atmosphere around Commerzbank was sheer terrific.

On the evening of the twenty fifth- a Friday, Stephen had been joined by an out of the blue Nicole as he strolled home from the Pep Supermart a couple hundreds of metres away. It didn't really bother Steve, it was her trade mark pattern and he had often teased her in the good old days of why he chose the bore of secretarial work over a sure detective job with the Metropol Polis. Of course, she never had no reasons- one could see that she enjoyed herself even in this mixture.

'What are you going to say,'she had asked. Stephen gave her a 'I don't get what you're saying' look. 'Common, what are you going to say on the podium.'

At that moment, it dawned on Stephen that he hadn't even given a thought about that. And he was hardly the eloquent guy. 'You don't expect me to rehearse for an award I have just a one in four chance of grabbing?' He gazed at her. 'Do you?'

'Humbler than thou, swear that you don't know you are the unannounced winner!' She teased him. In that moment, Stephen took her in. Her frail frame was decently covered in one long pink gown, her auburn-hair rested on her shoulders and although it was late evening, she was obviously as fresh as she had been since she came to work. Nicole was not overbearing in her make ups. She knew her strengths lay beyond her facial appearances and she worked hard to sharpen her dexterous mind. Tonight with less than two statements, they had fallen in stride and undoubtedly their minds in sync.

'Do you really think am gonna win this?'

'I don't think,' He turned around sharply. 'I believe.' Stephen grinned. It was good to have at least one person who believed enough in him. 'And a true winner is always prepared.' Nicole was catching up on her chance. Alas there was one thing the ever efficient Avri had forgotten to take care of.

They had strolled home ranting on what should be the content of the acceptance speech. He had barely three days and very little time to do the necessary.

'Don't tell me you are going to do a speech without appreciating me?' She sounded as serious as she was playful. Stephen swallowed hard. He had anticipated this part and he was just rehearsing the last part of his presentation. They were sitting on the broad creamy sofa in his sitting room, a few inches apart and in between rehearsals and corrections, they had taken the liberty to brush across each other and even slap hands. It was an unusually light evening- the kind that precedes an impending success.

'Nicki,' he only called her that when he was in some sensual mood and the last time was over two years ago. 'I don't think it would be wise mentioning your name here.'

'How could you say that?' 'We've been together and just-'

'That's the point. Acknowledging that fact is risky'

'Risky how?' She would always question even the obvious.

'Risky as in-.' He hurriedly wrote out the letters on the same page as the prepared speech was.

'I really don't want to get into this argument tonight.'

That was all it took for the mood to sour. A sullen silence ensued, discomforting considering the quick intimacy they had just enjoyed. Stephen was not sure what to do next but he knew one thing definitely, Nicole was never going to feature in his speech.

Nor was there ever going to be a speech for that matter. On the eve of the D day, Stephen had received a knock on his door. He was not used to unscheduled visits so he had stayed put on his bed. There were a lot of tiny threads sewn in his head and he had taken that night to really balance all of them. He loved to evaluate and re-evaluate until there were no more bumps in the plan. The knock had persisted and even gotten fiercer and he casually had gone to take a peep. To his amazement, there were at least three distinctly parked vehicles belonging to the Investigative Bureau of the French Polis.

Stephen practically ran to the door. He had never had any shave- close or far with the law enforcers and he didn't pause to wonder why.

With stern purposeful faces, they had asked him to accompany them to their office for questioning.

In three long days, Stephen could not lay hands on the intricacies of the challenges he was confronted with.

Nicole had been missing for two nights, he had agreed to having seen her on the night of her disappearance, confirmed that they had an unprecedented hot argument just before she bolted out. Stephen was being as honest as his conscience demanded and that was total but it took a whisper from a caring officer to inform him that he had better get a lawyer. The summary of what turned out to be a fruitless French sojourn was that the best Stephen could get was an instant deportation straight to Nigeria. His muffled offence was assault and near-rape of a French national. It was a sham of a trial. It really didn't need scrutiny to know that some high powered people were pulling the strings. He was just in the mesh of a grand plan. So, on the sixth of December, Stephen landed at the International wing of the Murtala Mohammed International Airport, an obvious wreck of a man. His lawyer made it clear to him that he would be lucky if he only got the deportation option as there were a string of other allegations of molestation threatening to open up. In retrospect, it appeared that jail was not on the option list of what they wanted to do with him. The dramatic changes crippled his appetites and left him with no desires to really challenge the allegations. How could he fight enemies he couldn't tag. Faceless people he knew they were not his people. He had spent all of himself pursuing economic improvement for a people who saw him as alien. He had nursed the ambition to return to Nigeria that December but of course not once did it occur to him that he could be robbed of all he had suffered to become. He was sent back as a moral pervert, indecent for co-habitation with whites and needful for rehabilitation or isolation. There was nobody to really recount his ordeals to; nobody would believe his innocence. To live was to Struggle. To survive was to rise. Stephen had painstakingly shown himself worthy among strange faces and bizarre cultures. He had nearly achieved that. Now he was dumped among his own people and it beat him how he was going to thrive. That was the first and only time Stephen stepped on the suicidal ladder. He did absolutely nothing to better his life. For over four months, he hid under the shadows of despondence- creeping in and out of his late parents' home. The apathy to life was beautifully carved on his face. His numbed mind darted from suggestions to answers in search of reasons why these things had happened. Perhaps he hadn't performed certain rites in the village and the gods were haunting him. Rites like having a proper befitting burial for his long dead parents. They had probably acknowledged his ascent in status and expected him to come fulfil that obligation. But there were no warning signs? Or had he been overtly insensitive to them? Was Nicole a sign? He felt he had successfully tamed their relationship out of sheer respect for the Chairman and yet, he had been scape-goated. All that he could have done to her or with her and he had given up, needlessly listening to a vague voice of reasoning. Should have, could have, would have enjoyed the moments of opportunity. Somehow, it struck him repeatedly that Monsieur Pierre was subtly involved in his catastrophic ejection. That was one mystery he was certain time wouldn't tell.

The lethargy had persisted until he stumbled into Bowono. Apart from meeting Julie, that was the luckiest encounter he had ever had with anyone. Stephen's rebirth had begun with that friendship. They were two friends who brought abstractly different strategies to the table. In eventful succession of years, the dejection stepped aside to untold affluence- the worth of which could make Commerzbank shudder.

Stephen pushed the paste right into the oven and readjusted the settings. He had been kneading for just over an hour with occasional pauses to recall some of the tips Bow had given him the night before.

'Knead until you can't feel the sugar in the paste.'

Bow's Instruction number eight of ten. He hadn't tasted the sugar grain in the paste so he had moved on.

'Set the oven timer at forty minutes at....'

His friend had mentioned a particular temperature but Stephen couldn't recall that. He simply studied the graduations on the face of the oven and turned the knob to sixty five degrees centigrade. If it was a mistake, he prayed it wouldn't rob him his result. He then calmly walked back to the sitting room where he was going to wait.

His subconscious yawned for a break- a nap but he resisted the urge. He had had a hectic day at the office followed by a demanding task in the kitchen. He prayed sleep wouldn't sleep his wait.

The second prolonged blaring of the horn jolted Stephen out of his drowsy state. He knew instinctually that his family was home, he hurriedly pushed his feet into his slippers and fled to the kitchen. His mind raced uncontrollably- swift bradycardia to tachycardia shift. As he approached the door, he stood still and drew in a chunk of air. That usually put some steady on him. The oven had automatically turned off and he hissed at himself, acknowledging that he had been asleep for well over the forty minutes. His heart was skipping; he should have checked the cake at the expiration of the pre-set time especially since he wasn't sure it was forty minutes Bow had instructed him. In any case, he abducted the oven door and the vanilla-chocolate flavour bumped into his nostrils. He smiled deep in his soul. The cake was ultimately well done. Stephen heaved in relief and re-shut the oven door. His entire household knew he was bad in the artistry of cooking. It was repeated at every meal how 'daddy couldn't even boil an egg'. That was equally part of his motivation. He needed to prove that he could do whatever he set his minds on- irrespective of precedents.

From the tail of his ears, he could hear the sound of tyres on gravel- that meant they were about a thousand five hundred metres away. He had pressed the ENTER button as he fled to the kitchen and from experience, Julie usually took eight minutes to drive from the gate to the house. She usually rode at thirty-forty kph and each four hundred metres had a stretch of different materials- from coal-tar to gravel to white sand to inter-locks. Stephen's trained ears could tell where a car was at every point in time.

He still had about four minutes to tidy up his surprise. A lavish spray of the rose-scented air-freshener in and around the kitchen and he sniffed around a bit stupidly for escape cake-scents. The room was drooling with the new fragrance so he shut the kitchen door and walked to the window to watch the car make the last of the turns into the house. He had stuck to his principles of having only the members of his immediate household in his home. Despite the huge difficulties it had earlier presented, his wives- Julie and Lucy had eventually learnt to manage the extremely flamboyant home without extra aids.

If their husband thought them competent enough to dispense their responsibilities, why wouldn't they?

A house as ambiguous as the Avri's would have seemed prone to crumble without a handful of gatemen, flower keepers, househelps, drivers and such likes but the Avri's had devised a way to effectively keep things trim. All hands were always on deck- working with a commitment that could only be borne out of love.

George, Zwitt, Julie and Lucy filed into the living room, their hands belaboured by the vast purchase they had just made. Zwitt and George clang to their toys while the ladies almost dragged in a basket full of beverages, ladies-things, flowers. Stephen took his gaze away. It was Julie's birthday and she was celebrating it in sheer grandeur. He had parted with a quart of a million to let her effect this spree and true to herself, she had quickly swung into action- A shopping for 'whatever you desire' for every Avri. Stephen didn't have to come with them but he could swear that he was adequately represented in those baggages. It was an evening full of promises- for very obvious reasons. Stephen took turns and embraced all of them. The little men were so excited that the hugs meant nothing to them- it was a distraction as far as they were concerned.

'I think I perceive something very unlikely,' Julie pointed out, immediately after her hug. Her nostrils were mysteriously twitched towards the kitchen.

'Yea,' Stephen explained. 'I fried some eggs to death- till they became a black heap.' He glanced around. 'The whole house was up in a stench so

I had to use the air freshener.' He stared into her eyes for some belief. It was unrevealing. 'Probably used an overdose,' he finished.

'Hmm, eggs?' Lucy just put in. Stephen stooped down and feigned interest in one of the bags. These women were not going to beat him to this game- not today.

Thirty three years into life and eight years as Stephen's wife, Julie was not an inch less stunning a lady as she was when Avri first set out to conquer her heart. She still had tales of young men stalking her or sending her love lines or gifts in spite of the certainly non-negligible diamond ring that screamed from her ring finger. Her slender height and shiny brown skin which thinned out as a flurry of gloriously silky dark hair did not help matters. She had a set of deep dark eyes that could effortlessly checkmate a biased judge and even till the moment, earned her unsolicited confessions. She had this weird reputation of being approached by acquaintances or even strangers with hitherto secrets of their lives. Everyone always wanted to share in her magical presence and she was hardly the type to snob off another. Notwithstanding, Julie's forte lay solely in her uncanny ability to correctly interpret latent emotions.

Stephen was aware of all these. It was almost routinely impossible to pull Julie a perfect surprise. She always would smell it, feel it, dream it- something it! Half surprises were literally better than none.

Lucy made to take some of the new purchases to the kitchen but Stephen saw her early. Three quick successive steps and he aborted her mission. At this point, he chided himself for not having involved the rest of his family- save Julie in his plans. How was he going to contend with two women with such arresting personality? Again, Julie saw the interception.

'Steeeeeeeve,' She had her trademark way of drooling his name. 'What exactly are you hiding?' She glanced at his brows. 'You are even sweating like you've been pounding yam the whole time we've been gone!'

Stephen grinned and wiped the sweat off with his gown. He only just knew he was sweating but who wouldn't be? These adults were too pushy and he could sense that his surprise was about to collapse on his head- if he didn't act fast and smart too.

Maybe there's a third wife in there. Lucy's cynical mind suggested. She chuckled to herself at the thought and tried to glance away lest someone read her mind. If someone was capable of that, it was only Julie.

'Birthday baby,' His gaze danced around as he searched for the appropriate words that could caress the situation. 'Is it really out of place for your man to use your kitchen just for a historic while?' he made sure he emphasized the 'your'. If he still knew his Julie well, the ceding of kitchen rights to her would ease her curiosity- at least temporarily.

'Stephen's history is never made in the kitchen. That we all know!' she feigned to turn to the kitchen. This time she saw the plea in Stephen's eyes. 'I really pray we won't be calling the Fire Service to this home,' she teased. 'Or have they come and gone?' She pranced across the roof in a mock search for soot or burnt ceilings. Stephen saw his chance and seized it. He placed his finger on Julie's lips and with the other hand, shepherded both women back into the sitting room. Lucy was more than eager to get done with the excuse-antic conversation.

'Now, if you ladies would permit me, I have got to resume duties right there.' He pointed at the kitchen. 'Why doesn't someone officiate the boy's match?'

Zwitt and George were already engaged in their typical wrestling contest, each mimicking the moves of his favourite wrestler. Tonight, Zwitt was playing 'The Rock' against his brother 'The Ultimate Warrior'. They would entangle, tumble and fly at each other- displaying a gloved version on what they watched on TV. Their bouts often ended without a winner- that's if it ever ended. Usually, the fights were swiftly terminated by Julie or Lucy- when it appeared the Ultimate Warrior was losing.

Julie smiled broadly into Lucy's silent stare. Where Stephen Avri was concerned, being up to something was always worth it.

The two Mrs Avris made small talk back to the sofa as an entirely fraught Stephen brisk walked to the kitchen.

The clattering from within the kitchen failed to drown the belated mood of the now three occupants of the sitting room. Julie and Lucy hadn't been seated five minutes before Zwitt abandoned the bout to lurk around his mother.

'The red gown would have been absolutely stunning on you.' Lucy was sizing up a hands-free Dolce and Gabbana pink gown that Julie had purchased this evening.

'Of course,' Julie agreed. 'But I feel I am gradually weaning off that my usual craze for dazzling colours.' She moved over to the small heap of cloth they had acquired just today as if to ensure that she didn't make any mistake of getting any loud colours for herself. 'I think Steve would love it,' she stated matter-of-factly. 'You could still order the red one if you really love it.'

Lucy nodded curtly as a flash of worry crept into her mind.

Why did Julie always have to personalize Steve. Now, she was telling her that he would love her-Julie on pink and with the same mouth, she was suggesting she-Lucy go get the Red version. Both of them were together in this and frankly, it didn't matter who was married to first. Stephen was theirs.

She scowled. *How she would have loved to use 'hers' in place of 'theirs' but then..Could Stephen Avri love both Pink and Red equally? Her doubts were rock solid.*

Julie notoriously read through her silence. She admitted to herself that she ought to have censored those remarks. Introducing any hint of bias at this hour was the last thing she would wish for.

'Lucy dear, I'm sorry for-'

'No, it's nothing,' Lucy replied rather hastily. She was embarrassed that she had let Julie read her mind again. To buttress her indifference, she waved her arms across her face as she kept muttering, 'It's nothing dear.' An awkward pause followed.

'Jayy, please I'll need you to help me convince Stephen.'

Julie looked up to rest her gaze squarely on her. ' I know as a matter of principle that we are not allowed to stay out beyond nine p.m and all what not but I really really want to be part of this Hinn's crusade.' Julie had seen flyers on the upcoming Benny Hinn Inaugural Grand Crusade at T.B.S Lagos. In fact the entire town was hyped about the giganticness of the crusade. It was as if Jesus was coming to town. The Christian kingdom was all over itself with the reality of bringing such renowned VIP per Religion to Nigeria, the small-scale business people were already scurrying for tents and market space. Even the sick were starting to queue up around the crusade venue and yet, the crusade was eleven days away.

'That's going to be a difficult one,' she glanced at the kitchen. 'Perhaps, we can ambush him in the euphoria of tonight. Persuade him to give us consent'.

'Us?' Lucy was surprised.

'Yea. Us!' Julie re-iterated. 'Did I ever tell you I was allergic to the gospel?'

In one simultaneous wave, their favourite 'That's my girl' line re-echoed and they gave each other a Hi-five. That was the magic of the Avri wives.

'Mommy,' Zwitt called, getting her attention expressly. 'How old are you?'

His voice was tiny and barred of excitement. He had been ignored since he crawled up to his mum's side.

'Mum is four years today,' Julie whispered as she stroked his hair.

Despite Zwitt's young age, he slowly shook his head. Apparently he had weighed Julie's assertion and found that age incredulous.

'Mommy,' he persisted. His tone hadn't changed even a note. 'How many years are you?' He really could ask the same question in many ways.

Julie knew his son was a die-hard inquirer. She had by no means expected her earlier response to settle the matter and he didn't disappoint.

Lucy idly ran her hands across her bulged belly. She knew better than to interfere in Julie-Zwitt bizarre networking.

Her son George had already fallen asleep on the couch- invariably exhausted to the marrows from the shopping and the brief game with Zwitt. *That was what a child ought to be. Gentle, subservient and malleable.*

'X plus One equals Y,' Julie repeated for the third consecutive time, this time winking at the undaunted Zwitt to lay off the question.

Zwitt recognised the expression on her ace and sadly went mute.

'Two unknowns make no equation!'

Julie sighed. Stephen had been following her conversation even from out of visual range. That meant the matter wasn't resting yet.

Lies always travelled faster- and on this occasion, louder than the truth; that was the only justification for Stephen to have heard her muted responses to Zwitt's nagging question.

'Don't let any other person hear that with all your vast exposures, you never stumbled upon the J-equation?'

Stephen blushed in quick resignation. Julie seemed profusely prepared for the day and he didn't wish to steal the joy.

No 9 Julius Nyerere Street Adejo Lagos was a sight to behold. Even in the engulfing darkness, it always shone forth into the lingering imaginations of anyone who had stumbled by it- anytime. Stephen counted himself hugely favoured to have triumphed in the site acquisition battle.

The then fallow parcel of land was strategic in its location and sacred to its owners. The land lay at the foot of the infamous Akorolo hill, bounded by intimidating rows of trees on all borders.

The contest for the possession of the land had been outright fierce- near fatal between the then incumbent Commissioner of Lands and Stephen. At that time, it was a remarkable mismatch considering the fact that the former had governmental authority at his beck and all of Stephen's worth was a pitiable fraction to what Chief Benson had amassed. Stephen had been resilient with caution in his bidding. He had been the first to indicate interest but suddenly, it didn't seem to matter. Several emissaries were dispatched to him to initially negotiate with him and then eventually warn him to desist from the contest. Just as the pressure became unbearable, events took a sudden strange turn. The Akorolo elders invited both bidders to a meeting where they had been fore-told that the final decision would be made.

'Our heritage does not call for such intense fighting,' the Akorun had declared. 'It is the same god who blesses a man that also run him down.' He was the traditional ruler of the people. 'We find it interesting that our land is held in such esteem by honourable men like the two of you but-'

His brief pause caught both rivals snaring at each other with palpable hatred.

'- I must tell you the myth behind the Akorolo valley,' he finished. The Commissioner shifted uncomfortably on his seat. He hadn't fathomed that he had left his pressing official duties to listen to tales- especially from the lips of a stark illiterate. Stephen kept his straight face.

'You must be informed at this point that there is more to this our ancestral treasure than crosses the mind,' the Akorun had concluded with. He had just fed them a half an hour epic story.

Both men were visibly shaken. Stephen could feel the sweats welling up in his pants. Now, there was an entirely new dimension to this desire.

If what the Akorun had just told them was fool-proof, he must be insane to want to desperately acquire a land that had sipped in an innumerable volume of infants' blood. The valley had been sacredly designated as the sole centre for the wasting away of the lives of twins and congenitally deformed babies. The practise had traversed the years and had not too long ago been terminated by the in surge of foreign beliefs and religions. The land had subsequently been cleansed and declared free by the new generation Charismatic Christians.

'Mr Akorun,' Chief Benson addressed the Akorun. He wasn't

concealing his disregard for the traditional institution. 'I do not wish to suppose that you think such stories can dissuade me from my quest.'

He was just warming up. 'I am a man of proven worth and it beats me to think that no one in this kingdom has been kind enough to whisper into your ears what your people stand to enjoy if I invest here.'

The Akorun did not alter his countenance. He simply glanced at Stephen to hear if the latter had anything to say. With Benson's display of arrogant bravery, Stephen whisked away every fear the tale had instilled in him. He resolved to fight to the end. If the decision favoured him, he could pay and quickly re-sell.

'The decision you have come to hear,' His voice was different and distant- like a relay of some divine message. 'Had long been made by the gods. It was just a matter of time before they revealed it to mere mortals.' His stern face settled squarely on Stephen. 'You have been chosen to inhabit the Akorun Valley.'

Chief Benson had stomped out of the meeting but not before he had rained a barrage of threats on everyone who had connived to steal him of his dream acquisition. Stephen sat still, confused and short of what reaction was more appropriate for the occasion.

As time told, Benson's threats weren't in any way empty.

Two foiled fire incidents at the work site, a near smashing of his head by a mysterious block and a successful robbery of his construction store jolted Stephen to employing utmost caution in all dealings as regarded the erection of his palatial home.

In all, it took Avri three full years to bring the master-piece to completion- in spite of the abundance of resources.

Incredible. Stunning. Unthinkable. Those words were not alien to his ears as an array of admiration plunged in after the house was declared open.

'Sometimes I get the feeling that those gods have got some sense of cash.' Julie had teased after Stephen had rendered her an edited version of the Akorun's tale.

'I think it's a fairly cheap acquisition.'

If Julie had the faintest idea that the issue was beyond figures, she would have done everything to dissuade their building on such land. Stephen had engaged the project with cautious extravagance and indeed monumental intensity. It was an outstanding epitome of a master Architect's ultimate effort- the sort he could rarely ever reproduce.

As work progressed at lightning pace and strangely invisible results, Stephen had often had to resort to Julie's eye of faith to believe that they were on track.

They wanted so much squeezed into their home. So much so that they just had to be patient. She was right after all.

Their castle was gallantly flanked on all sides by fifteen feet fences and three ten-feet gates in between- as though the owners were making frantic efforts to shut out the historic evil and retain the flux of peace within its confines.

The Akorolo hill was likewise wrapped in by the fence and its flora and fauna were quarantined to suit domestic presence.

No.9 Nyerere Street was infallibly always the last to receive of the sun's setting gesture and in an aesthetic vision, it seemed the hill endowed lingering sunlight on the castle even till the late hours of the evening.

'Darling you are keeping us nervous,' Lucy complained. There was no trace of bitterness in her voice.

'I suppose I am the nervous wreck,'

The women chuckled and Julie burst into a hearty laugh. Someone must have made a joke and she was relishing it.

The unsuppressed laughter moved Stephen to smile. He was an extremely fortunate fellow. Polygamy, the admitted doom of many a great man had dealt him ten-fold blessings. He hadn't imagined he would be the type to gamble with his marital future- not with the discord he had seen in other trial marriages. But then, fate had pressed him and right now he couldn't tell whether he could have chosen any better.

Discretion- that inept wisdom that crept up in his life time after-

Stephen jumped inches to his left, instantly returning from his daydream. The broken plate splashed all across the floor of the kitchen. This was the second time around and he had hidden the crumbs of the first carefully. Now- another one.

'Ewoo. We can hear you,' Julie laughed on. They had heard the shattering sound.

Stephen whistled loud as he tiptoed to get the sweeping brush.

'By the time you finish, we would have just spoons and forks remaining.'

That is if he was staying one week. One thing that he had done wrong was wearing the flowing gowns into the kitchen. It was Julie's most recent gift to him and by tradition; he always wore the latest gift he had received on her day.

He was getting jittery again and he stood still and drew another deep breath, steadied his grip and briskly set the cake on the tray, the knife harmlessly laid by its side.

'The triumphant entry into…' He let his voice trail.

The march was nothing short of triumphant. Alas, he had his own cake on his hands. Just two steps away from the kitchen, the feet long knife slid rudely off the tray and landed on the floor. Stephen did a reflex mini hop and then watched the knife dance briefly to a halt a few inches away from his right foot. Mr Avri masterfully held the tray on his left palm, stooped over and picked up the knife. He still had a quarter of a century metres to walk so he lodged the knife into his massive breast pocket. He couldn't afford to gamble with anything falling off at this time. He proceeded on his snail-paced journey.

'Not too far off now.' His head popped out.

'Yes. I think I perceive it. Yes!' Julie shrieked. She was most responsive to cakes and chocolates.

Stephen blushed. 'It's not exactly as beautiful as you are.' He wondered if Julie had smelt that he had a chocolate cake in the offing. The intensity of her excitement sent shivers down his spine.

'Common Steve, anything from you can't be less beautiful.' Julie's eyes rammed into Zwitt's. Those young watery eyes had been fixed on her for some minutes and she had struggled not to acknowledge them.

A pair of partly frozen and somehow watery eyes meant surrealistic things to her. Her prior composure swiftly disappeared and an itching guilt overwhelmed her.

'Baby, mom is thirty-three years today. Would you now be happy?' it was her innate unspoken answer.

She confronted the idea and then resisted the urge to speak. Perhaps she would tell her later tonight. As for now, she just drew him close and parted him on the back.

'-making it so gruelling,' Lucy half-whispered with a faint touch of irritation provoked by the extensive suspense.

'You haven't told me you would love to see it,' He was still lurking against the wall.

'Of course, you know we would,' Julie answered on their behalf.

She stole a quick glance at Lucy and then extended her free hand to clutch hers'. Stephen was undeniably pushing their anxiety but she was responsible to keep any intolerance in check.

Lucy warmed up to her touch.

'Ten, Nine…won't you all join me?'

Julie, then Lucy picked up the count down as Stephen reluctantly emerged- back to audience. Julie watched Zwitt for a while. His lips were parting and shutting as they formed the digits but no sound came off his larynx. There was a tiny pool of tears building on his lower eyelids. It wasn't the first time she was noticing it and against her optimism, it often struck her as symbolic of tears awaiting shedding. *Tears for whom?* She had never found a perfect answer.

Zwitt was her only and ever feasible issue- heir apparent of the Avri Dynasty. The toils of having to sacrifice such tons of blood and very nearly her life for the birth of a single soul had sown the strings of inseparability between Mother and Son.

Four years into existence and Zwitt knew his mother like the back of his hands.

Julie clutched Zwitt's little hand in affection or mysteriously for the fear of the unknown. Fear truly deserved to stay out of context but always and again, it fortuitously trickled within her.

Lucy's seamless inclusion in the family occasionally worried her- though unduly. Three years of co-habitation in unprecedented tranquillity did quite little to dispel her fears. Lucy had already bore George and was securing her stay with her present pregnancy. Securing was an abrasive word but it appeared comfortable on the night. Between both of them, Julie couldn't tell who was luckier. Lucy had been Stephen's avowed pre-sojourn fiancée while she was his welcome back package.

After their marriage, a confusing cascade of events had followed with Lucy's shadow looming strong over their union. They had eventually struck a compromise- This.

'-three, two, one!'

Julie broke off her thoughts to add emphatic delight to the 'one'. Stephen Avri noted with glee the tremendous surprise on each of the faces. Those expressions gave him some satisfaction. At least, his elaborate approach and his 'J' shaped chocolate cake were making their marks.

'A chocolate cake for my honey,' he drawled. 'You are indeed my everything.' He gazed into Julie's dark eyes.

Nobody heard Lucy's silent hiss. *If Julie was his everything, what then was she?* She was getting pissed off.

Julie was touched by Stephen's last remark. She ignited her pose and began to stand up.

Stephen in fore-knowledge carefully placed the cake on the nearest side stool and braced himself.

He wouldn't mind baking repeatedly just to receive an embrace of such genuineness. He broadened, then relaxed his chest- a finishing tape for Julie's emotional half-run.

'Stephen darling,' She leaned into his ear. 'Anyday, anytime, I would want to be your wife.' She was already choking in tears. 'You make me feel so heavenly.'

Stephen smiled into her face. Such moments in marriage weren't very frequent in spite of the bliss the Avri's enjoyed. He simply pressed her closer and more intimately.

The sharp grunt that followed shook everyone up. Stephen loosened his tight grip and to his shock, Julie slumped. A gory sight of blood was the least anticipated scene in the household. A stream of blood seeped through Julie's clothes unto the floor.

'Mommy, Mommy!' Zwitt's voice re-echoed throughout the room. He was already beside her and the rapidity with which her pupils bleached stunned him.

Julie turned towards him as her mind queerly wondered on what the most befitting final words for a dear son.

'Thirty three' ricocheted within her senses but it didn't seem to tally with anything reasonable. She warded off the thought knowing just as well that she lacked the strength of speech.

The realisation that she was being torn away untimely from the people she cherished didn't bother her any bit. In its stead, there was a refreshing wave that blew across her mind. Her dimming eyes rested on Lucy as her hands pranced across her limp body. A trim measure of scorn was tucked in somewhere in her face- behind her ears; or so Julie thought. She was too calculated to pass without suspicion.

Julie beheld his son again and her heart skipped a painful beat.

As Julie slumped, Stephen had quickly caught her before she hit ground. Everything had turned sour in a flash. He had understood the joker immediately Julie had shrieked in pain. Ideas deserted his mind as he felt everywhere for the pulse- the jaws, the elbow, the wrist. He was berserk as he watched her ebb slowly away. Julie didn't seem to take notice of him even at this last hour.

The cut was ugly and deep; the knife had entered through the apex of her heart and its trajectory had most likely severed a pulmonary vessel. The accursed weapon had of course torn through his breast pocket and done its damage in a most gruelling order. A kink of teardrop appeared on the corner of his left eye. It was his left eye that cried whenever he was terribly shaken.

'Stephen, aren't we going to do anything?' Lucy asked with ruse worry.

The cold voice dazed Stephen. Lucy had as a matter of a fact returned to her seat. Stephen nudged at his rising fury.

'Not with you sitting tight over there. Can't you see I need a hand?' he yelled.

You need more than a hand. Lucy strolled back to where Julie's lifeless body lay.

'Please, Lucy call Dr. Ariwe- Zinny Hospital,' Stephen instructed. He really needed to think more clearly. 'Ask them to send us an Ambulance.' He needed to think much more clearly. 'Get the car.'

Lucy kept her ground for a couple of seconds more. She wasn't sure what instructions she had to obey. Zwitt was wailing and tugging at his mother's arm.

'The keys?' She stalked about the sitting room for an *hour*. That was what it seemed to be in Stephen's mind. 'I think they are in Julie's bag and-'

'And what, Lucy?' Stephen screamed back. She was shocking him with the attitude.

'And you know I can't search her bag without her permission.'

It was a joke and coming from an adult, it was a bad joke. Further weighed against the prevalent circumstances, it was a fatal one. Stephen sidestepped her and got to Julie's bag, emptied its content and grabbed the keys.

'I think I should make the call rather,' Lucy mumbled as she excused herself.

It was neither a request nor could it pass for an exact statement. Stephen stared long and hard at Lucy's shadow as she disappeared to make her call.

Zwitt was still kneeling aside Julie's body and his father gestured that he made way for him to carry her into the car. Stephen refused to see the hopelessness of his cause. People didn't just die like that.

'There has been a murder,' Lucy was weeping into the phone. She glanced behind her to be sure Stephen hadn't crept up behind her. She was safe. 'There has been a murder, Hello…' She wailed louder. She had been the lead performer in 'Solar'- their theatre group in the University.

2

8.40 p.m. A.Y. Rizi yawned for the fifth time. He clumsily cupped his hand across his mouth- seconds after the yawn had fizzled out. It wasn't his fault- that was when he typically remembered it. The distant voices of the few men in the cell made him glance up from the counter, in the direction of the cell. His Birds of virtual captivity. For a while, his ears had followed up on their discussions. It had been mostly arguments- fierce but seemingly docile topics- punctuated with low inaudible whispers. No matter how hard Rizi strained his ears, he failed to pick those troughs in their conversation and that frightened him. Miscreants were often the same- always fluctuating between loud cheery moments to frightful wimps of depression.

A.Y Rizi hissed in disgust and wilfully retracted his ears from his 'colleagues'. He really thought them so. They were behind bars, he was behind the counter- none of them could go anywhere-at least for the rest of the night.

Adejo Police Substation was nicknamed 'The Desert Station' and in many people's opinions, correctly so. It was a station that had everything going against it- the staffing, the inmates and the structure. It was hastily erected about seven years ago as a final resolution to the perennial dispute between the Nigerian Police and the Nigerian Railway. Both government agencies had laid claim to the land and it had taken the building of the station to crush the discrepancy. It was a slap on the face of the Railway management of the time but they had swallowed their vexation and moved on. It was a most unstrategic position for such a building but the damage didn't stop there.

Perhaps in the rashness of the decision, they had forgotten to include such basic rooms like toilet, clothe-swap and bath. Staff of both sexes had to seek such luxuries outside. With time, the omission began to seem justifiable.

The Desert Station was that 'single voice crying in the wilderness.' On any ordinary day, one could completely effect a change of clothes outside the building without fear of being spied upon. There was also no provision for water hence both officers and inmates had to stroll some distance to pass waste or bath- the latter under armed supervision. Asides the preset free-to-air times, any inmate who wished to pass faeces had to seek alternative methods- sinister, unhygienic means. As such, this break period was a daily eagerly awaited fiesta.

The morale of the Policemen around the station depleted with the passing years. The spirit always was at a perpetual low and despite occasional efforts made by the Head of the Regional Station to rekindle passion, the station only had space for officers with bleak ambitions.

In healthier and busier stations, it was undeniable that there were officers who prayed and hoped that they would switch stations. For such, the Desert Station was their luck at its crux.

No matter how many nights A.Y Rizi did, he still hated doing nights with a passion. He was starting to feel vague and alone. He didn't need to check the time; he knew himself outside in and by practise, he rarely could keep his eyes open beyond 9.00p.m. He dropped the three year old copy of the monthly journal 'Crime Watch'. He had been reading the same journal for two years now and each time, he hardly finished a paragraph. The seventy-three pager never seemed to finish. He smeared the outside of his left palm over his eyes and for the twenty fourth moment today, he cursed himself, his profession and his existence. Even while asleep, he had a store of curses for the trio.

Born Azu Yosi Rizi- forty three years ago- to what he deemed the most poverty-riddled couple. A.Y Rizi had never been able to free his imaginations from the clutches of such amplified penury. His parents for undisclosed reasons had given him names as fluent as a Rockstar's. Azu Yosi was not a name one would forget with ease and irrespective of his inferior attitude to life, he was often called up- sadly for the wrong reasons. He started early to blame his parents; the instant it struck his consciousness that he was the only pupil who trekked barefooted through the rings of paths that led to his elementary school, the sole pupil who latched on to his books like they were firewood or sometimes he stuck them under the grip of his armpit.

His thoughts ran a circumscribed route through out those early years. Even now, they hadn't changed course- they only ran a little faster.

Why me?

Young Azu's disbelief in himself and his cause for existence reached enviable limits. The prospects of achieving anything worthwhile had never struck him even for a moment. He groped through his early education, graduated into the streets and even there, the chills and thrills of the streets offered him little succour. He was a born mediocre; scared stiff of challenges of any shape and size- either confrontational or imaginary. In the same measure he was scared of success, he shirked responsibilities.

A.Y Rizi- Beautiful name, scanty future. His anatomical build was another let-down to him. As though his inadequate height wasn't enough headache for him, his once-upon a fine face had received an unfair share of tiny lifelong pimples. Of course his head hadn't been the exact size for his rather small frame but he used to get along fine until puberty knocked him out. It did hurt him more, each time he saw those same spots erratically displayed on his father's rapidly shrinking face- a bold reminder of how he would eventually look. Trouble.

His enrolment twenty years ago into the Nigerian Police Force was just about the best decision of his lifetime- he was certain he wouldn't make any better one. At least, he was on a salary roll and it didn't seem to perturb him that twenty years after, he was still stuck at Sergeant A. Y Rizi. His ineptness to mistakes, numbness to sensitive issues and his trademark dumbness were orientation benchmarks for any new recruit to the force. He was the ideal man to talk to when any of his colleagues desired to vent their heavy heart and expect nothing but nods and hisses in response.

Azu heaved in distaste and undid his shirt's buttons. Despite the barrage of surrounding trees, the night was unusually hot and he didn't need debriefing to know that if he desired a good night rest, light dressing was a prerequisite. He neatly placed his shirt on the vacant seat his colleague- C. O Yemoya should have occupied.

C. O was just another one. In so many ways, he had resemblances to A. Y but history had shown that unlike the latter, he usually took square blame for his mistakes- as often as they came- and then he would inadvertently repeat the same errors. By mutual consent, they had forged a reputable partnership; silly to the core. Tonight Yemoya had persuaded Azu to cover-up while he strolled into town to warm his newest girlfriend's bed. A. Y knew every side of the story. The girl in question was a plantain-chips hawker who C. O had dramatically helped to recover some long-standing debts. The debtors were a couple of road-side mechanics who according to the complainant had threatened her and verbally assaulted her. Yemoya had been touched- more by the raw beauty of the girl than her reports.

He had only had to wear his uniforms and exercise his bulky frame at the mechanics' and all the cash was quickly provided. And how much was that? Seventy naira! In any case, he didn't stop there. Yemoya was not the marrying type- at least in his own mind. The young girl was new to the streets, was nineteen but had the looks and innocence of a fourteen year old. The ravenous policeman could smell that she needed protection and he had it. So they naturally stuck.

A. Y Rizi swallowed the saliva already filling his mouth. He couldn't help imagining what C. O would be doing just about now. He smiled at the thought and shook his head. It was certainly not good for a man to be alone. But not on this count, he liked being on duty alone.

Off the records, it was a mystery that each time Sergeant Rizi manned the station alone, no distress calls ever came in. He was the only one who knew his secrets.

A.Y glanced at his wrist watch. Twenty minutes gone past nine. He was five minutes late. Without much ado, his hands reached out for the telephone and just as he felt it, the telephone rang. The shock of the surprise caused him to retract his hands; as though he

had just touched a hot oven plate. He was overwhelmed by a combined wave of fury and irritation. That five minutes delay was his bane but the degree of the consequences was still uncertain. He hesitated and prayed the phone would go dead.

Tonight, he was unfortunately not in heaven's good books. After a vain wait, he raised the receiver.

'Yes,' he bullied. 'What is it?' His voice was stern and gruffly.

'Please,' The intruder was a lady, he noted. 'Is this the Adejo Police station?'

'Woman, I should be asking you.' He paused. 'Was it the Adejo Police station you rang?'

'I'm sorry,' the quiver was unmistakeable. She sounded like a woman in dire trouble. 'I am Lucy Avri-'

Her voice tailed off. Rizi sincerely hoped she wasn't waiting for the name to click recognition. He could hear a couple of suppressed sobs in the background.

'Please I need you to send your team over here.' She stopped again and when she heard nothing from the other end, she continued. 'Sir, don't you understand? The address is…'

Again, Azu's mind trailed off. *Why do people always have to encroach on other people's lives? What made this woman- whoever she was, believe that her life was more precious than his?* Nothing was worth more than A.Y Rizi's good-night sleep.

'- I think there has been a murder.' He heard her finish. What excellent dirge! He was absolutely unmoved by her pleas. For a second, A.Y weighed his options. He could simply hang up or just keep dragging the conversation in masked confusion until his intruder's patience waned.

A silent voice chipped into his thoughts, 'What if it was your wife?' Until then, he hushed it quickly.

'Woman, you are missing a fundamental point.' He had chosen the latter option. The Nigerian Police Force is a well-established arm of the Nigerian Government. You may not know it but it was inaugurated in Nineteen Sixty Two.' He paused to make an 'am I sure' face to himself.

'Before Independence, there was what we call-'

Lucy was totally livid. She had listened quietly to the babbling until now hoping that the policeman was on the verge of making a vital point- towards sending of a rescue team. At this point, she was certain this man was mad.

'What's wrong with you,' she flared up. 'How could they put a jerk behind the desk? I am telling you-'

A.Y was the officer solely-in-charge. He resolved to stamp his authority.

'Madam,' he cut her protest short. 'The police was not instituted to understand what people to think. Why don't you call a Psychologist?'

'What?' Lucy screamed back.

'I said that here we act only on facts- precise and true facts, not on fragmented thoughts of people. If everyone was to call in with his epileptic thoughts, what do you think we would become?'

'So, what are you trying to say?'

Good question.

'Why don't you continue staying alive while I work out the modalities of getting a rescue team across.'

A series of frantic gratitude followed and Rizi waited for her to finish.

'I will send you a team as soon as we establish contact with any.'

He heard her heart capitulate. It was apparent they both knew the truth- there was never going to be a team. Not now, not later.

'As for now,' he concluded 'God is totally in control.' He quickly replaced the receiver. His last statement had come as a shock to even him. Trusting God was not by any means his style but he had just preached it. Maybe, there was a God factor to the night- otherwise why would the name inadvertently creep into his speech. He reached again for the phone and dislodged the receiver.

At long last, he shut his eyes and leaned further into his world of untrammelled peace.

3

11.30a.m. Sunday. Bowono Jereny unleashed his bulky frame on the sofa and as expected, the sofa shrieked in helpless agony. He had just woken up from a supposed 12-hour sleep; seventy percent of those hours he had spent pondering. Now fully awake, the worry was boldly encrypted on his face- a sharp contrast to his usual gay self. His eyes had no business being open so he shut them again and wished away the incidents of these recent days. Futile.

All his comfort, peace and security seemed in a desperate hurry to elope.

Bow had woken up to very loud persistent bangs cum knocks on his door. Before he glanced at his bedside clock, he was innately vexed in the spirit. What intruder would opt out of using the door-bell and stamp on his door with such ferocity. It reminded him of his land-lady – back in the years. Then he saw the time- 11.20a.m. Lucy had called in earlier in the wake of the night to tearfully request that they see. He had given her 11.30a.m. She was certainly one of the few who would dare hit him up like this- and the mood justified her too. From the moment he let her in to now, she had barely said anything. Her chronic sobs and wimps spoke for her. Tears streamed down her eyes and every time Bow dared stare into them; he felt he saw a desperate plea for deliverance. Everyone seemed to have suddenly changed. Lucy –by Bow's assessment- was never the one to break down easily. She had a backbone of sheer steel and even her husband had often jokingly referred to her as 'one full woman, half a man.' In short terms, Bow knew her as One and a half. Of course, she didn't know that; those were strictly men's talk- done over sealed contract papers and excellent wines. Today, she was a shadow of something else.

Bow returned his gaze to Lucy's face in frantic search for something crocodile-like in her actions. Her eyes were genuinely welled up with tears and her complexion seemed to have mottled a little bit. She was a woman in elaborate agony.

If Stephen had done as she alleged- in their tele-conversation yester night- there was truly a cause for everyone to sit up. The curtain parted a little and a refreshing dose of breeze swept across his brows. The cold feel suddenly made him aware that he had been perspiring. Jereny's head dropped. If he could stop believing his guest, if she could just give away her hither-to intact credibility.

'What do you think would have caused AV to kill Julie?' he asked dolefully.

His mind was already skirting. He had known Stephen- whom he called AV- for almost six years and in that huge span of time, no matter how thoroughly he searched, Stephen had been just and dear to him. He had never met him begrudging or brooding heavily over any matter or anyone.

But people sometimes change, he pricked himself. For a reason, he added. Even then, Stephen couldn't arbitrarily decay into the psycho Lucy was narrating him to be.

'I don't know…I don't know,' Lucy repeated amidst her sobs. There was so much pain in her tears as she curled herself further on the couch directly opposite Bow's. By now, she had cried for so long that her cloth was duly soaked in both sweat and tears.

Lucy's choice of cloth was no mistake. Before she left home, she had carefully mapped out every little act in her performance. She knew she had an adequate stock of tears to move even an impotent sadist and she understood that a bulky fraction of her success today would depend on her ability to generate sympathy. She had worn a cream coloured silk gown, armless and boldly knee-shy. In her crept-up stance, the wet cloth strictly outlined the meagre fraction that it was supposed to conceal. Bow took a stride closer to her and tried to console her.

'It kills me to imagine why life is like this,' she swallowed hard. 'One day you are obsessed with someone and the next-' She lowered her voice and with the most bitterness she could muster, she added, 'you dispense of her.'

Bowono shrugged subconsciously as she read between the lines. Lucy's obvious fear was that she could be the next victim, right after Julie. There was no rhythm to what a disintegrated mind could do. It could even be him. Time was of the essence.

'That evening, Steve was totally strange. First, he wouldn't go shopping with the family- a deviation from our annual family tradition. Despite Julie's intense persuasions, he didn't budge'

Bow's mind was racing still. Stephen had shown an unprecedented interest in baking and although he had gone ahead to teach him all he required, it had never occurred to him that it was part of Stephen's grand plot towards executing a dastardly act. Yes, it was queer for AV to suddenly want to bake and- . Bow's mind jumped. Did AV seek his tutelage just to get him mixed up in the whole scene? It had better not be.

'If Stephen truly wanted Julie dead, why did he have to hack her down himself? In the presence of the entire household?'

'That is part of my confusion really,' Lucy cried. 'That innocent boy- Zwitt, he has been in shock since then, hasn't been able to utter a single word but am sure,' Lucy was practically wailing as she 'relieved' the incidence in her mind. 'Am sure we can caress him into confirming all I already told you.'

There was a reflective silence. Both were briefly lost in their ship of thoughts.

'You can imagine how gruelling it is for me,' she sobbed as she searched her handbag for her handkerchief. The clattering of all the stuff she had earlier packed into the bag distracted Bow for a while. He made an unnecessary attempt to discern which sounds belonged to the near empty perfume bottles Lucy always carried. It was an odd time to recollect this but all the same, he recalled Julie once joking that Lucy would never let her perfumes finish.

Meanwhile Lucy continued to grope inside the handbag. She knew she hadn't put any hanky inside there. 'I know my husband is your best friend. He is also the best man I've got and my soul-mate too.' She paused. 'but believe me, this is not the Stephen we once knew. Something sick has seized Stephen,' she ended on a wail. Bow nodded softly, fetched a napkin from wherever and offered it to Lucy.

'Here, use this.'

Lucy mopped the welled ears, slowly and almost unsuccessfully. Fresh streams of tears still oozed out. Her gaze was firmly fixed on Bow. This was the last stanza to her act and so far, she hadn't disappointed herself.

Bowono Jereny couldn't lift his gaze off her either. His testosterone levels were on an all-time high. It seemed like the rudeness of recent events had also hyped Lucy's wild beauties.

His senses were choking him. His discipline had long given way and he found himself labouring to draw from the pool of respect he had for Stephen.

A sudden urge to believe this lady gripped him. He had to offer her some security- in any way possible. He was lucky to be still single or was she the lucky one? Bow smiled sadly. No wife would ever accept this degree of seduction in her home- panic-struck wife of best-friend or not!

Lucy wasn't slow to observe the remarkable changes in his host's countenance. She was a trained eye- experienced enough to detect lust especially when it came nude. She pretended she still had some untold sections to the story.

'He spent nearly twenty minutes lurking behind the walls, apparently putting final touches to his plans. You should have seen him as he fooled us from one pre-amble to another until he was ready.'

Bow's hands were already half-cupped on her neck, creating some form of dam against the hitherto free-flowing sweats and tears. Asides her initial shudder when his palms first hit her skin, she didn't seem to bother.

'We all trusted him.' His fingers drew faint rings on her neck, the fluid serving as lubricants. 'No one would have imagined that he had other plans. Julie died in utter shock- after the likes of Julius Ceaser.' Bow lifted her with absolute ease. She was an easy carry despite her bulged belly. Destination, bedroom.

'Bow,' she whispered just before he laid her down. 'When someone you trust hurts you, it's like a,' she searched for the most appropriate word. 'first death'

Bow nodded. *I will give you the First resurrection.*

'You just have to let me take it from here. If Stephen thought he could get away with this, he must be a joker.'

Lucy smiled. A weak tired smile that seemed to suggest 'Here is my man.'

'He will be put away for a long long time.'

She wished he had said 'Forever' but whatever was the case, she had found a gullible believer at least.

Picking up the disarrayed cards one by one took Zwitt a minute and forty three seconds. Though his hands traced the edges of the sofas for the many cards that were off his perimetry, his thought s had long veered off from the parlour and were skidding with pace down memory lane. He really didn't need any concentration to reshuffle the cards and he wasn't wasting any either. Today he was examining his life.

He had become a terribly neglected victim of fate; Conned by the mother, ignored by his father and brutally intimidated by his step mother. He had rapidly receded into an alloyed wreck. And not that anyone seemed to notice.

Zwitt retrieved his thoughts, shoved his ass nearer to George and began to share the cards. Both were seated on the tiled floor in a portion of the sitting room and George's back rested on the couch behind him. There were four 'conclaves' in Stephen's parlour. Each had its own settee, designed in a unique fashion.

There had actually been five until tragedy struck and one was compulsorily deleted as part of the effort to erase memories of that ugly night.

Zwitt sat just opposite George. His eyes were defiantly narrowed as they followed Zwitt's distribution of cards. After the last game- which he had lost as usual- Zwitt had promised him a 'three card-less' advantage. He was eleven months younger than Zwitt, looked exceedingly more healthy and consequently older. His temper could frighten a wolf and often times, he was attitude-rupt. He was the loudest voice in the household- spurts of quick, careless speeches repeated especially when he was in his mother's company. When George cried, they were usually repetitive phrases, beckoning on inanimate and animate things. Sometime last month, it had been screams of 'Mercedes', re-echoed into the stillness of the night until his father intervened. Stephen had had to auction off his newly acquired Mercedes S class. Lucy at times feared that he was genetically malformed- a suppressed imbecile but she wouldn't accept such thoughts. Not her son; not an Avri heir hopeful.

In spite of George's verbosity, it was either stone silence or a one-sided ranting when both boys were together.

There was no animosity. Their fondness for each other was only evident outside home. Right now, George's patience was under threat. He had lost six consecutive "whot" games and this last time, he had furiously flung the remnant of his cards into the air immediately Zwitt said the imminent cum ominous 'check-up'.

'You think you are going to win,' George repeated everytime Zwitt played and he went to 'market'.

As the current game progressed, George made all the faces his five year old sense was capable of. The facie didn't help his cause. Zwitt's cards were reducing at lightning speed. Again, Zwitt flaunted his expertise and George for the second time flung all his cards into the air, stood up and fumed into Lucy's room.

Lucy lay face-up on her bed. She didn't feel like siesta but despite herself, moments like this were her most fertile periods. As her eyes slid from one ceiling board to the next, her thoughts waxed stronger and even appeared to gain direction. She typically made a mental note of where everyone would be right about now.

Geria- her little daughter- was visibly asleep on the baby's couch just by her bed. She tried to recollect whether she had eventually worn her the pampers just before she dozed off. Stephen's 'no house-help policy' would soon ease out. It irritated her each time she had to change soiled pampers.

George was playing cards with that idiot in the parlour, his bowels would be ramming and hopping by now. All thanks to the stench that came off Zwitt. Idiot Senior would be somewhere in town, winding down the remainders of his free days. He would be surprised at how times had changed everything. It wasn't really time. It was his stupidity that turned everything around.

Bow- her man, would be at the office. Probably sorting out the last of the necessary documents. He had assured her that they needed a lot of paper swindles in their favour before they could strike. She trusted him. More importantly, he trusted her.

Julie? She hissed. Julie shouldn't be a question. Wherever she was- Lucy was so glad that she didn't stay long enough to warrant her having to kill her herself. They would have eventually come to that.

George bumped into the room- of course without knocking. His manners were not missing. He never had any.

Lucy studied her son's face as he weep-narrated why he was throwing tantrums. Her son deserved better than Zwitt gave.

'Wickedness,'

George glanced up to his mother. 'Do you know what wickedness means?'

He shook his head innocently. Her pat stabilized the shaking head. *Basic knowledge or rather The Absence of Basic Knowledge.*

'Gee,' she began. ' Wickedness is when you leave..' she broke up. '..no, abandon the people you are supposed to love. As my baby, it's my duty to be here with you, directing you and showing you all the love you need.'

George nodded. He loved it when his Mum spoke in parables. He knew he wasn't expected to understand much- unlike those horrible exercises in school.

'Zwitt as you know, once had a mother but she chose to abandon him.'

George nodded in arbitrary recollection. He had a mother he could rely upon for anything.

'That was just one of the many wicked things she did,' she chuckled. 'And as you see, wicked mothers bear wicked children.' She raised her voice a little. 'Wickedness is when you won't let others have a taste of what you have.'

George was absolutely confused. Wickedness was becoming many things all at once.

'When you win and you won't allow others win- even once,' she added sternly. 'What will you call it?'

'Wickedness!' George confirmed. Everything today had to be about this big word.

Correct response. Lucy patted him again on the head.

'Now, we can't always stop wicked people,' Lucy noticed George's spirit capitulate. 'But we can hurt them.' His mood rose again. 'We can pay them back by destroying things that are dear to them.'

'How mummy?'

'Show that idiot that it pains you.'

There was only one idiot in the household- at least to the best of his knowledge. He smiled, turned around and half-jogged back into the sitting room. He was grossly transformed.

'Can we play again,' he tenderly asked Zwitt after he had picked the cards. Zwitt opened his eyes. He had fallen into a fatigued sleep on the floor. He was fortunate it was George that woke him- not his mother. He glanced across the room. George had picked up all the cards.

'We are starting on even cards this time,' he announced as he shared the cards.

'Are you sure you can handle this?'

'Sure. Why not? Mom says I have to learn how to win from losing positions.'

Zwitt smiled into his blush and they resumed play. The game wasn't any different. George threw in the wrong cards, made the wrong demands. As usual, his strategy was a mess but there was something different about his attitude. It was unusually volatile- like he didn't care again whether he won or not. In less than three minutes, Zwitt did it again.

'I warned you. You can never beat me,' Zwitt laughed into his brother's seething fury.

George smiled humourlessly as he slowly got up. He had anticipated this moment or perhaps longed for it. Throughout the brief contest, he had searched the span of the sitting room for something 'dear' to Zwitt. What could make the wicked cry? His eyes had eventually descended on a valiant option- just as Zwitt said 'check-up'.

Just about the same time, Stephen pushed his tired legs down on the throttle of his 'only' car. The highway lay bare before him and his BMW

Obiora Oji

responded hungrily to his demands. That was why she qualified to be called his 'only' car asides eleven other fine cars. Eleven or twelve, he had even stopped counting vanities. He glanced at his rear-view mirror- no other car was in sight. His baby car was just about four months old on the Nigerian road but it seemed to navigate like it was designed for these roads and by extension for him. He couldn't imagine anyone else behind these particular wheels. They bonded at first drive. Stephen sank further on his seat. A pot hole daringly came into focus. He swerved frantically, a mad rush of adrenaline filling him up. His reaction was good but a little too late. The screech of his tyres rang into the still evening as his car took to the tarmac.

'Gosh,' he heaved as he brought to car to rest. He was lucky there were no oncoming cars. The screech had caused a handful of heads to turn towards him. He put his car back into gear and returned to the road. He needed no extra piece of bad publicity. What was all his hurry about, he mused. He admitted he had been unleashing the frustrating pressures he felt inside on the car.

Bow had called him only ten minutes ago.

After the usual pleasantries- which were becoming unusually strained in recent days- a rather strange silence crept in.

'Steven,' Bow had broken the silence. Stephen took a mental note of the 'v'. It was Bow's usual way of showing discontentment. ' There is so much going on right under your nose and if you asked me, I think we need to get together and talk.'

'What do you mean by beneath my nose?'

'Right under your nose. The part you can't see without a mirror or a friend's help.' He added emphatically, 'Sadly, you've been avoiding both.'

Another silence followed. Bow seemed to contemplate telling him his mind over the phone.

'8.20p.m tonight at- '

To Err is Woman

'That's late my friend,' Stephen snapped. 'You know I've got a family to run back to'

'Forever's,' Bow finished and hung up.

Whatever evoked this sense of brash finality from Bow must be pretty consequential. He had no memory of anyone hanging up the phone so rudely on him. Bowono was his best friend- the only way he could trust his back with. A lot had truly gone down since Julie's death. Threats of court charges, ritual-making stories, outright rebuff by some business friends. Tough times. He was a tough man. He brushed aside what was left on the table and picked his car keys.

As Stephen crawled on the road, it occurred to him that he hadn't even given a second thought to the appointed venue for the rendezvous. Forever's. Cold chills ran through his body.

At the end of the sitting room, George paused and looked back. Zwitt had withdrawn his attention and was lying prostate on the sofa, awaiting the chariots of sleep.

Lucy's disciple noiselessly tiptoed to the dining area, lifted one of the dining chairs and returned to the edge of the parlour. He knew just how short he was but his thoughts ran deep and high. This night his thoughts had caught up with a framed portrait of Julie. It was a four by three feet chef-d'oeuvre, placed another three feet above the ground.

It was undoubtedly Julie's finest picture and even after her demise, her genuine smile still entranced the house from that position. Anyone who dared to stare into those still eyes always felt more magic- always.

'..destroying something dear to them.' Lucy's voice ricocheted in his tiny memory. He was certain he had found an adored one. He had often seen Zwitt stand in awe before the portrait. It was almost a daily ritual.

Despite his best stretch, George couldn't reach the frame enough to bring it down. It was then it occurred to him that all he needed to do was just to unhook it. With the tip of his middle fingers, he pushed the base of the frame up. He was successful at the third try. The glass frame crashed down while George rested his eyes on Zwitt. He wanted to see the pain at onset.

The loud bang woke Zwitt up and he impulsively turned to where the sound emanated from. The sudden realization of what it was that had just been smashed. Everything seemed to freeze for a few seconds. Even George was surprised at the response-lag. But when the reaction came, he saw it a fraction too late. Zwitt made a decisive leap toward him, seizing him just in time before he could descend from the chair. There were splinters of broken glass on the floor but they dared not prick Zwitt. He raised his right arm to give George a virulent slap of life. It never landed.

In a flash, Zwitt's outstretched arm, his head and his entire body ran circles in his brain. He had never felt a pain of this magnitude and spontaneity before. He quickly retraced his steps as he writhed to the second descent of the koboko. Third lash and he was sprawling on the floor. It was only then that he could lift his eyes to know where the punishment came from. He also saw George peeping from behind his mother- some glee tucked in those eyes.

Corporate pain, Lucy told herself. *Wound the spirit, Sting the flesh.*

Lucy shepherded her son back to her room. She was extremely pleased that George had found the nerves to accomplish today's feat. That portrait also worried her too.

'Make sure you sweep away all that rubbish before I come out again,' she yelled from inside the bedroom.

There was no use whimpering. Every single day without his mother taught him that everyone had only one mother. And he had lost his.

4

Forever's was not the kind of place a man of Avri's principle and class would want to be found. As he pulled up into the parking space, his eyes roamed its whole breadth and his auto-evaluator pointed out that there was really no vehicle that came close to his. A grey Honda Accord salon car was the best he saw. Two 504 peugeot cars parked beside each other as though to offer mutual support. Perhaps there was a special space for more exotic cars; it couldn't exactly be ruled out. As long as the tariff was exploitative enough. Lagos always made provision for everyone- only at different costs. Bow's minted Hyundai was also nowhere in sight. Stephen peeked at his wristwatch, a 48-carat Rolex that usually trans-illuminated at first glance. Then he pulled it and placed it into the pigeon-hole. He didn't need any extra stares inside. He had to look like the regular guy here. He unfastened his seat belt and thought better of sitting to wait for Bowono to arrive.

It was possible the more prudent Bow would rather come in a taxi that subject his car to treacherous eyes and palpable insecurity. These Forever's folks had to do something about their security- if they wanted to retain clean patronage. Of course, the notoriety of its clientele seemed to help sales- one way or the other.

The place hadn't changed a lot since his last visit. He had actually vowed then- under duress that that last visit was going to be his last. And he had kept his word until today. A few 'furniture' faces and he had to check his gait to double his chances of anonymity. The arrangement of the bars had also been altered but they had kept to their colour identification codes. With the growing alcohol stench in the air, an overhanging signpost showed a different shade of red. It always got redder with the farther in you got. Of course, there were bouncers and club administrators per inlet. Stephen had never gotten to the tail of the club. He didn't bother either. He usually found a seat after the fourth shade of red. That way, he reasoned he wouldn't be sitting with or risk being disturbed by club mongering riff-raffs nor would he be with the very wealthy hard core criminals.

Almost eight years ago, just before he tied the knots with Julie, he had made the impressive mistake of bringing her here. It was a spontaneous decision. A club to wow her- she hadn't been to nor even heard of Forever's. At that time, it was the most perfect error to make. Alas, she had given in to his persistent requests to blow her mind at Forever's. They had been seeing each other for ten months but the visit almost arrested their relationship.

Not that anything huge happened on the night but between both lovers, the uneasiness on her part grew into latent fury. She was embarrassed to say the least as her eyes flashed from one pant-less waiter to the braless ones. He admitted within himself that for the first time in countless outings, he had taken his fiancée to the wrong place.

Forever's was the crème de la crème for all blends. There were no strict dress codes but everyone knew what to expect. Strings of sexually explicit girls thronged around serving drinks and more importantly themselves to the guests. It was another marketing strategy and the owners knew that an aroused man would spend happily and incessantly. The club had a round the clock appeal. It always looked like dusk inside its space and the excitement expectancy was always on the rise. It had made semi-addicts out of ordinary men like Stephen and eventually Bow. They usually did at least two Fridays in a month in the good old days. Stephen wasn't sure whether Bow still came around here. Chances were in the affirmative, otherwise why would he make it a venue.

As expected, some sexual adventure also laid in their records.

To Err is Woman

Until Julie visited.

Although she didn't need to say a word, she had unequivocally said her impression.

'Stephen, I don't think I would be coming back here again,' she said at the end of their hour and half 'clubbing' cum puzzle fiesta. That was her perfect style. She was hardly assertive- even as her eyes told Stephen the rest. *And be sure you too aint.*

Anyway, her thoughts stuck.

8.44 p.m. Stephen sat at a corner, sipping his soda and observing the entropy around. His own internal disorder stifled any libido. The whole dark hall danced around him and it seemed it was only he that sat calmly- not dancing nor nodding to the noise overhead. It used to be music- not so long ago. Inside, Stephen Avri was by no means calm. His heart tore to shreds. In the masking gloominess, it was only a chronic 'been-to' who could discern objects and faces. Stephen had luckily or sadly found the same spot he had sat with Julie empty so without thinking, he had sat just there. It was a vintage position, he could study the entire proceedings without being awkwardly noticed. But it was an epileptic study. Excerpts of that night with her came in-between.

Stephen recognised Model. Unconfirmed sources said she was as old in Forever as the club was. She had adopted the title after uninterrupted years of service at the club. She had seen hookers come and go. No-one really bothered about her real names. She had a fine figure- a subtle reason why Stephen had assumed she bore the pseudo name. She had been utterly jobless and with miserly qualifications, she considered herself fortunate to have been recruited at Forever's. Age was no longer on her side but she had garnered experience- enough to still keep her relevant to her employers.

Stephen frowned into the darkness. Model had spotted him and was walking straight towards him. They were old pals but lifestyle was not in their favour anymore.

'Mind if I joined you?' Stephen was jolted. He had been absolutely pre-occupied with Model's analysis that he didn't notice the stranger sneak up to him.

'I'm with someone,' he replied spontaneously shaking his head. He had thought his positioning offered him some immunity from these lose ladies.

The lady scowled and instantly moved on. Stephen peeped further into the darkness. Model had also changed destination. Hookers here never loved contesting for clients. His eyes trailed after the departing lady. Her waist swung in all planes- a dream girl in the day time and a hooker at night!

He shook the last traces of soda in his tumbler and then gulped it down. 9.12pm. Stephen was a little anxious. It was atypical of Bow to make false appointments at all, not to talk of with him. Some respect was eroded. He knew Stephen valued his time like his life.

He darted his eyes around the hall and after a futile search, he ordered for a second soda and rested his head on the table. He felt the waiter drop the soda on the table but he neither raised his head nor opened his weary eyes. His eyes were sore from watching the erotic images and from looking out for Bow.

He promised himself a little more patience before he would leave. Calling Bow's line was not an option he wanted to entertain.

He perceived someone withdraw the opposite chair and then place something at that tangent of the table. The person sat down lightly and gasped wearily.

He could swear it was Bowono.

'After a hard day's work, bees barely have time to enjoy their honey,' a richly feminine voice began.

Stephen believed he had dozed off. A sweet seemingly familiar voice. Something said about honey. *What was it he had told Julie about honey? Honey was a bad omen.* His mind sped in the wrong direction. Images he had shut off- wit intense labour- flashed across his mind. He closed his eyes tighter and waited for the dream to cease.

'I know you are exhausted,' the voice was saying 'but silence shouldn't be the answer right about now.'

Always suggestive. Never assertive.

Stephen was scared. He was afraid of lifting his head and seeing the wrong person. He pretended not to have heard.

A few more seconds passed. 'Sir, are you alright?' There was unmistakeable worry in the voice now. She had reached across the face of the table for his hands.

Stephen lifted his head slowly, his neck bent at an angle. His heart throbbed uncontrollably. He did a perfect job of concealing his anxiety.

The intruder wore an out of place suit. That was his first impression and Stephen smiled inside. At least by appearance, she didn't seem 'clubly'.

She retracted her caring hand as Stephen straightened up on his seat.

A small ovoid face- the size of one of Stephen's palms, pointed nose, crystal clear eyes and precisely tailored teeth. Her mouth was agape as though to flaunt her exquisite dentition. There was sincerely nothing suspicious about her personality. She was a young girl- maybe in her mid-twenties but she appeared to have long matured. Her expensive wine-red well-tailored suit stood out even in the near darkness. Yet, everyone seemed to be uninterested in her presence.

Still, Bow was not anywhere close. The handbag stood curtly on the table. Stephen relaxed a little.

'I am perfectly okay,' he said flatly. 'kind of waiting for someone.'

The lady blushed. Her disappointment glowed.

'I am deeply sorry for invading your privacy,' she reached for her bag. 'I hope she hasn't spotted me this little while that I've been sitting here.'

Stephen waved her worry away with a grin. She didn't look any bit harmful.

'Common, it's not what you are thinking. My friend would be surprised to see us together but then- we are talking about a he, not a she.' The clutch on the handbag eased and the apologetic face waned.

A little too quickly, he observed.

'Stephen Avri,' he introduced as he extended his hands for a handshake. Her palms were syrupy and almost too soft- another indication that she was a 'botty'. Stephen's rather rigid grip seemed to crush her fragile hands. As they withdrew their hands, he thought he saw red ridges on her palm, through the dim light.

'Aswa Totle,' she said queerly, after the handshake. Her 'it's my pleasure' was drowned in Stephen's.

A little silence followed as each evaluated the other. Stephen hoped she wouldn't tie his name to nothing just yet. He had made tragic headlines over a year ago but she didn't seem like whom he should hide his true identity from. When she didn't come up with the upstart 'Stephen Avri, Stephen Avri'- They always repeated the name as they tried to tie it up- he calmed down. Friends were best made neutral.

He was appreciably rusty in the art of making sheer friends. Recent years had been more about making clients out of strangers. Of course he was well versed in the trade of wooing potential clients and marketing all he wished them to swallow. These clients would hardly ever turn to friends. They were strictly business associates.

He was stuck on where to resume. Then he remembered that Aswa had towed his line in the introduction.

'Mrs or Miss?' he asked coyly.

'Mrs.'

'That is to say you are ma-married?' Stephen stuttered. This time, he betrayed his surprise. 'I mean, you certainly don't look it.' He attempted to make-up.

A 'that's to say I look irresponsible' frown hung on Aswa's face. Stephen recognised it with some effort.

'Please excuse my rashness,' he whispered. 'But in all honesty, you look too innocent for a been-to'

'Been to where?' Aswa cracked up. 'Is that what you call married folks?' She kept on laughing. 'I swear, have never heard anyone describe it in those words.'

The hearty laughter instantly dispelled the almost rising tensions. She really knew how to laugh.

Stephen nodded in rhythm with the soft music from the old block. It was Lionel Richie's How Long. She joined and even began to hum. It appeared like some divine forces were already orchestrating this encounter. Again, they split up in their respective thoughts. They really had said very few words. The lyrics had come in handy when he had been on Hard to Crack Julie's case.

The way she hummed it, he could decipher it meant something to her as well. They were silently settling seamlessly.

'This is one hell of a club,' he heaved after the song ended.

Aswa nodded. She had no idea why but she was grinning from brow to cheek. It was her first time here so she had no premise to agree or disagree.

'So what brings you here? Business or the other?'

'Neither, I regret to say.'

Stephen waited for her to elaborate at least a little further. She didn't seem to have even considered that. She was thrifty with words and they were sheer strangers, he reminded himself.

'Forever's is not the kinda club you just stroll into for nothing.' He emphasized the 'nothing'. 'Unless if you are a journalist?'

'Then it would be work,' she replied. She seemed to be searching the hall with her eyes.

Stephen raised his eyebrows to reveal his confusion.

'It's always Work in Progress for a journalist,' she explained. 'But I am certainly not one,' she finished throwing her hands up to protest her innocence.

Stephen motioned the bar-tender to their table. They always had a pseudo-aggressive poise whenever they noticed an empty table or empty bottles. This particular had been standing innocuously but questionably about three feet from him. His Curiosity was starting to build and he was willing to unravel this mysterious lady tonight. A little red wine would perhaps ease her a safe notch.

'Make our orders,' he asked her politely as the waiter arrived.

'I don't know your brand yet and you are-,' she froze in mid-sentence as her eyes guiltily fell on the soda bottles on the table.

'Take a wild guess,' Stephen teased. He had drawn his conclusions. Only an outstandingly dull journalist would miss those bottles in the time they had had. She was not a journalist. 'Who knows, it may come as close as it gets.'

'Two Chapmans.' The waiter turned to go. ' Wait, and a Jack beside them.'

Stephen was bemused. This one was a rebel. He wasn't going to waste precious time courting a rebel. Not at this stage in his life. He flipped his phone open and tried Bow's number, despite himself. A monotonous voice spoke into his ears. Bow was not reachable at the moment. He could drop a message after the tone.

Rubbish, he slapped his phone shut. He resisted the urge to show his frustration. A list of harsh messages were at his disposal, yearning to be voiced out but he felt it would be a little inappropriate letting this stranger into his irritation. He would parry until she was gone. He hissed mutedly and pushed the phone into his pocket.

Aswa observed him closely. Her soft gaze was not by any means soft on the prior-to very composed Stephen. He was visibly uncomfortable. He was starting to sweat and they were even yet to start.

'I get the feeling you are nervously waiting for this friend.' The Nervous was heavily pronounced.

'That's not true,' Stephen denied. His eyes roamed the bar. 'I am just being careful should your man appear with a jealous bottle on his hand.'

Aswa chucked.

'Jealous bottle indeed.' The waiter was almost within earshot. Stephen shifted on his seat. What was he going to do with a Jack Daniels?

He heaved. 'I frankly don't want to return home bleeding. He has enough reasons to explode.'

Aswa smiled lightly wishing Stephen's fears were genuine. The waiter was laying the drinks before them. Stephen's mouth gaped as they placed another soda before him and a glass of chapman in ice before Aswa. *When did this woman alter the orders or had Forever's devised a code for drinks that he wasn't privy to.* His anxiety soared although he was glad that there was no damn Jack on the table. There was something about Aswa. Retreat was ruled out for him.

Aswa sipped her drink. Whether Stephen liked it or not, she was bent on steering their conversation to the waters that would justify her venture. She already knew a handful of truths but her mission was strictly confirmatory.

'You don't cut the picture of a coward though,' she appraised him. 'However, one year ago, this assertion would have been absolutely correct.'

Stephen barred his relief from showing. He wasn't sure what to feel but he knew smiling would be most foolish.

'Considering your looks, permit me to say that you threw in the towels quite early.'

'You mean divorce?'

Stephen nodded. Aswa's gaze left his face for the first time. Slow tears tricked down her cheeks. The sudden onset, non-sob associated breakdown stunned Stephen. He was lost.

A wave of cold breeze swept across the room. It was probably an omission in the usually sealed air-conditioned bar. He glanced at the windows. They were all shut. He was afraid he was starting to have fever-chills.

You should have shut your dirty trap, he rebuked himself. *Now, here are the worms you have just opened its lid.* He was still clueless when Aswa spoke.

'I'm sorry for that,' Aswa's tear-soaked velvet voice interrupted his worries. 'I really thought I had grown stronger with the passage of time.' He wasn't getting her drift.

'I just couldn't bear the suggestion that I divorced Kim'

'Please pardon my arrogance.' 'I know full well that some wounds are best left undressed,' Avri apologized.

Aswa raised her hand to tell him not to bother.

'When you are drowning in the grief of a lost love, paddling with the strength of memories; neglect only makes you sink fastest.'

Parables. That was one of the many things Stephen had little patience for. Unknown to him, Aswa was well debriefed.

'Stephen,' she hesitated. 'You mind if I call you Steve?'

'Of course,' Stephen answered without thinking. 'Do you mind' was his most confusing English phrase. Most times, he was so confused with the implications of either responses- No or Yes- that he had devised the 'of course' answer. That usually threw the bait to the other person to act as he understood. His ears were yearning for her story. She seemed to realise that too.

'It might sound strange Steve but exactly a year ago, at about this hour- my Angel was sitting on the same seat you occupy now.'

Stephen blushed. He didn't like what he was hearing. He didn't believe in unprovoked coincidences. People didn't have to make their histories around the same objects. *Well, same position but surely not the same seat.* He found some comfort in that. The club cleaners must have joggled the seats over the months.

'Kim, that is?' he asked mechanically.

Aswa nodded as she continued her tale, her voice rising and falling with palpable passion.

'Love really meant little to me. Something that guided my childhood fantasies but the older I became, the more it dawned on me that love was one virtual enticer of appetites.'

Her fingers lined the rim of her glass as she recollected more painful details. Stephen wished he didn't take this turn.

'Kim was my last straw at loving. I truly had no expectations of him. He was to do like his predecessors- catch the fun off me until he got exhausted and called it off. It had become a pattern and I didn't expect anything better. But he started off differently, showed a selfless level of commitment like I had never seen. Gradually, he wiped away my pessimism and in its stead was a strange desire to make this one work.' She paused as though to clear her head. 'I didn't just want it to work, I wanted it to last forever. He defined everything afresh for me. Love, Life, fun, discipline and marriage; the companionship was extra-terrestrial.'

Stephen knew where this part of the story was leaning dangerously to. He also knew what finding Love was. He had touched the skies, flying on Julie's wings. Those wings, that flight...

Aswa stopped to gulp the remnants of her drink. Her demeanour buttressed the bitterness she was feeling. Stephen felt all the more sorry for her. The last thing he desired- a dirge- had befallen him and all because he had pulled the wrong strings. He had no choice but to listen to the rest of her heart-wrenching music.

'Please take my soda,' he offered pushing the drink to her end. Perhaps, soda could sober her up. She muttered a thanks and kept her silence. Stephen was in turmoil. He wanted to hear the rest of the experience. *What exactly had happened? Beautiful love turned sour. Routine Nollywood practise. Change of Love?* He wanted to know how the Angel had ruthlessly ripped her heart.

'Asie.' She looked up, genuinely surprised. No one had ever called her that- not even the fabricated Kim.

There was a supreme warmness about him and she hadn't been

fore-warned of his serpentine side. She shuddered. Duty first. Still her heart skipped on. The man that was dearest to her called her Aswy. It always sounded like Ask why and although she answered to the calls, they secretly annoyed her. In her senior secondary school days, it had been the 'Ass' saga. She had madly fought that to a hush although she knew they still called her 'Ass' behind her back. Her backside truly didn't help matters. Over-bloated firm protrusions that usually stood out whenever she wore her uniforms. The first teacher who had heard the 'Ass' phenomenon had taken it rather personal. He had taken the case to the authorities and it had sparked a debate in those years about whether the school uniform should be adjusted to free gowns. The male teachers were most-threatened by what Aswa and her likes welded. In the end, they summoned a handful of them to the Principal's office and instructed them to lax their skirts to appreciable degrees.

Here he was, a supposed stranger charming her. The beautiful thing, she agreed to herself, was not quite the name in itself but the manner with which he had called it. His teeth had trapped the tip of his tongue in a super-seductive stance. She had to be wary.

Stephen saw the different shades of expression race across her face just before the faint smile finally settled. He was encouraged. 'Where did it all go wrong?' he asked gently.

'In the real sense of the word, we never did go wrong. We never could,' she declared. 'Kim and I had two love filled years of mutual exploration. We were so into each other that we felt immune to the world and its tragedies. It was like we believed that the world was hinged on how much and how well we expressed the love we had.'

The sadness stole her voice briefly.

'Then the world had to teach us never to side-line it- the sad realities of living in it. Beautiful things, beautiful times and people don't last any long.'

Her face seemed to ask him, 'Don't you know?'

She let him digest that one. His curiosity was still screaming at her.

Aswa knew her storyline was superb- an any day thriller. The remaining bits of the story were exceptionally clear in her mind.

How she had persuaded Kim to mark the second anniversary of their engagement when it had just been a week after they celebrated their first year of marriage. The event had been done in the presence of close friends- imaginary ones. The story was designed to take a twist at the point where Aswa's friends had decided to leave just after midnight and their car had stubbornly refused to come on. At her persuasion, Kim had agreed to drop them off.

She knew where she was going to observe deceptive breaks in her story for effect's sake and what to do next should Stephen seem not too moved by her upcoming gruesome tale.

Her tear-tank was just below full capacity.

She resumed her narration again and by the time it got to the section where the tanker suddenly rolled across the road towards their speeding vehicle, she was sure she could read the horror on her audience's face.

With emotion laden gestures, she told him how Kim had heroically swerved the vehicle to ensure it was his own side that wedged the monstrous tanker.

'Kim's blood splashed all over me and-'

'Christ!' Stephen was in awe. It was a horrendous tale- made more real by his own experience.

Aswa's eyes locked into his. He could swear she was about to ask a really deep question.

'Steve, have you ever lost someone you loved with all your heart, your might and your strength?'

Stephen's world froze.

5

Lucy slowly opened her eyes to the intrusive network news anthem. The 9p.m news had just been concluded and she had heard nothing beyond the headlines- all thanks to the irresistible claws of sleep. She was a rare audience and had only lingered on the channel as it struck nine because she had hoped to hear some sad breaking news that would concern the only unaccounted member of the household- Stephen. Maybe a ghastly accident involving a BMW. In fact she wished it would be so bad that the reporters would only be guessing what car it was. Of course, she was disappointed and she paid them back my dozing the rest of the news away.

Instinctually, she knew it was 9.59p.m. That was when their age-long anthem blared to announce the end of the news. She wondered how most men sat through-out the torture, running unsolicited commentary as series of blurry images came to view. In the good old days, Stephen would curse at a certain government official who had done what only he and Stephen knew. Both wives would just exchange glances and sneer. Sitting beside Stephen as he listened to his nocturnal news was simply routine. They understood nothing. Indeed, they heard nothing. She shrugged.

Those were not in any way 'good old days'. The good days were now. She could speed through all the channels at wish and be sure nobody would dictate or contest. Absolute power was the *koko*.

Despite the loud creaking of insects, Lucy still thought the night was strangely quiet. She wondered how to pour some energy into the night. She got up from the couch and strolled to the kitchen. An opaque curtain of dissatisfaction hung inside her. She preferred to call it Ambition. Crawling up the irregular ladder of life had scorched off a measure of her femininity- a huge measure actually.

Lucy Obialuwagaeriakunnaya Nwoye had never had it easy from birth. Memories of her childhood always gave her goose-pimples. Not many people understood the rigors of being the last of a mutually unskilled and unemployed parents eight children. It was true that while the wealthy gave birth, the poor proliferated. That was the only explanation to Mr Nwoye's excesses. Two episodes of romance with twins didn't do him much good either. And he was not the type to give-out any of his children.

At four, Lucy had become conscious on what rung of the social ladder she had fallen into. From underneath the Ekure bridge in Ogun state where their home was, she and her siblings had turned to bread-winners at that very tender age. In retrospect it appeared his father had actually had a long term vision of raising a string of beggars hence he impregnated his wife at will. Bowl in hand, they navigated across cars held-up in traffic, making faces at wound-up glasses and reciting pleas for financial help. As typical with such trade, they often found a need to change business location as dictated by waning support or seeming over-familiarity among the locals.

In the absence of traffic jams, they usually darted to the nearest markets where they often employed a confrontational tactic. Their clothes were trademark tatters and without any second thoughts, they launched at unsuspecting pedestrians. Their rough but clean hands would suddenly grab passer-bys and cling on until they blessed them. It worked like magic in the first few weeks and then people started to avoid them. They would jog on, cross to the other side of the road or kick them away. None of these antidotes discouraged them. Perhaps that was where she learnt tenacity. Eventually, it took the intervention of the Local Government Authorities to expel them from that area. That day, the authorities had flooded the whole area and unknown to them, traced their every move. At the close

To Err is Woman

of work, they had tailed the breadwinners till they returned home- Under the Ekure. Just as they presented the proceeds of the day's work to their accountant- Mr Nwoye, they had swarmed in on them. Anyone who was just passing would think they had come to arrest a most wanted criminal. For her father, it was his second clamp down in three years. The Lagos State government had declared him persona-non grata about three years ago. This time, before his kids and wife, he was bundled alongside them and swiftly relocated in the dead of the night.

They were dropped at the Onitsha Head bridge in the early hours of the next day. From bridge to bridge, Lucy had thought in her naive mind. They were making progress. At least the new bridge seemed bigger and wider. She dreamed of more opportunities.

There was nothing exciting in being the little daughter of beggar parents but after all those years, Lucy could agree that there was something inciting nevertheless.

Her family had stuck on, hoping for nothing and believing in living out each day at a time. Despite Lucy's age, it grieved her heart to see her elder sisters waste away.

Martha, Oluchu, Angie and Derbie. They were in her eyes, too pretty to be her parent's kids. But there were an atmosphere of contentment in the home. No one ever stood up to their omniscience father. At least until Martha turned fifteen. She was the oldest of all eight and Lucy noticed a sudden strange light in her eyes. She was getting more and more disagreeable with their father. The dissent grew from muted ones to near outright quarrels and although Martha suggested no alternatives, it was clear she was fed up with the status quo. She wasn't willing to beg her adolescence away. She had started the under bridge parole since she was five. The stiff string that enclasped the family was under threat. Her father would have none of it. They had found a home on the streets and he wasn't going to let anyone delineate the boundaries of his hold on the family. It never occurred to him that the kids needed more than he offered.

He had taught them the rudiments of living and by the standards of their immediate home, they were well off. He hung on to his principles hoping and wishing Martha's rebellion would suddenly vanish. If his expectations ever stood a chance to come true, destiny didn't let it happen. Three of his children- Angela and the latter twins had mysteriously been swept away by flash floods as they slept. It had been an unusually rainy day and they had had almost no business throughout. At night, it dawned on them that a significant portion of their territory was submerged so they had to do an intra relocation. The male twins had been allotted a choice spot by their father; he didn't waste a moment to always show his favouritism to his only male issues. Lucy-though the youngest had gotten a space just by her mother. Her mother was just another one. It was hard to decipher whether she had been this conventional from birth or had been intimidated into submission by her husband. On the other hand, it was faintly possible that she loved this man so much that she showed this love by absolute submission. Well, on the night Lucy was glad she didn't get any favours. Suddenly the father had sprouted up to the flashes of lightening and deafening thunders but he had woken a little too late. All trio had been swept away as he had unwittingly placed their mat on the path of the flood. It was the bitterest moment in Mr Nwoye's life. His real children were lost in a moment out of his own recklessness. The shock didn't wane with time. The master tactician, beggar classico was defeated for real. For three straight weeks, they just mourned their loss. No work, no usual squabbles in the evenings, just long drawn faces. Lucy couldn't remember both parents ever sitting to discuss on any matter. It was then that Lucy realised that his father even had a saving. They didn't work yet they fed like they usually did. It was a plus for the father. They valued the break but it didn't assuage Martha's growing sense of self. Her father wasn't putting up much opposition either. The dysfunction nibbled at the family for weeks going.

    Lucy silently adored Martha. She wished she had the size or voice to lend her the support she sure required at that time. Martha's strength of purpose fascinated her. To others, their demigod father was as dangerous as he was silent. They waited for the rivalry to climax.

'Lucy baby,' Martha had called her. ' Do you know Christmas?' Lucy quietly shook her head. She wondered who it could be. She knew Martha, Derbie and Oluchu and the other one- Benedicta. At that age, she was not able to call her name to the fullest. It was always Be-be or she would rather address the ones with the easier names as she pointed at Benedicta. It was worrisome that Martha was asking her about someone else.

It was their last conversation.

'When I return, I will get you Christmas gifts, toys like other kids enjoy and many other things you will love.'

Lucy had looked on. She understood the 'get you' language but the issue of returning wasn't quite clear.

Her confusion was however erased the next morning. Martha was gone- taking with her the two decent clothes she had and as far as their father was concerned- her troubles.

The first tragedy, their father had grieved in silence. The second one, he didn't have quite enough time to grieve. That night, he had returned home smelling rather strangely of alcohol and then summoned the mother. It was the first time she was seeing their father furious and to think that he was directing it at the most docile woman on earth- their mother. He screamed and called her names for raising rebellious monsters as daughters. Her mother had replied with tearful silence. The tears infuriated him further. He landed the woman a slap. Lucy smelt danger, disentangled herself from behind her now wailing mother and went to sulk behind the only bunk in the arena that served as their house. The elder sisters stood aside and watched the drama. It didn't take Lucy a lot to doze off. Her thoughts had righteously dwelled on why an innocent woman would receive the brunt of a failed family. She had felt the father should rejoice at Martha's elopement rather than play the blame game. She didn't realize their father needed to set examples for the rest of the daughters. If they were hoping to grow up and contest his authority, they could as well back off out of sympathy for their mother. In any case, there was not going to be any growing up for them.

As providence would have it, it was the same sleep that saved her life. A raid of Under-bridge hoodlums had resulted in exchange of fire between the police and the criminals. The rest was unreported tragedy. Six casualties in one family. Only her little cocked head was spared the sedating splatters of bullets.

The sight of the rest of her family sprawled in their own blood had numbed Lucy. Their lives had been cut short just like that. Even her mum seemed to have been felled in mid-yawn as her hands were partly cupped to her agape mouth. Those images haunted her daily. She had been left alone to make her own mark.

She gulped down the second glassful of orange juice and slammed the fridge door shut. With it, she shut off further reminiscing. She knew someday, she would revisit these memories in full but for the moment, the past had to step aside for the present. No, for the future.

'What about the present?' her accusing mind asked her.

'Are you blind? That is what I'm working out!' she challenged it back.

There were few holes she still had to plug- and quickly too. She needed more people to believe her. The emerging story was a stark contradiction to Stephen's painstakingly built reputation but she believed in her powers to achieve great things. Nature was on her side, she was on track.

She replaced the glass on its rack and went to fetch her diary. How would Stephen feel if he realized that after this long while of marriage, she was yet to memorize a single digit of his cell phone number. She had also refused to save the number in her phone yet she knew Bow's number by heart. It was her resolve not to know Stephen's. Her life was larger than any god-damned marriage.

If Aswa noticed the fray in Stephen's countenance, she didn't let it show. Instead she reached for her handbag and searched for her handkerchief. With that brief search, she simultaneously set the tape recorder's tape rolling.

Then, she carelessly placed her bag closer to Stephen's end and wiped her stagnant tears away.

From the corners of her eyes, she watched Stephen fidget and regret.

Indeed, Stephen regretted towing that line of conversation with Aswa. Of a million and more topics, they had begun on a classically delicate note.

His throat was brittle and he was sure Asie could see the spirit drain from his face. He had to start somewhere, he had to say something but right now he couldn't evaluate his options.

'I' m really sorry. It's apparent-'

'No, no,' he quickly interjected. Again he was lost on how to start.

'Tragedy seems to have found us out,' he eventually began. Aswa kept a passive face. His tongue was ready to wag and she couldn't afford taming it with needless remarks.

'You see,' Stephen's eyes were running. 'This is the first time I am having to discuss this under such emotional conditions.' Aswa wondered but she knew better than break his thought train. 'Talking it over with a stranger even makes it more difficult or should I say- graver.'

'I am not a stranger to you anymore.' She couldn't restrain the defence from coming out.

He ignored her protest. It was like his mind was on a single lane, screeching and speeding down.

'Happenstance has never appealed to me really and even as surreal as our meeting tonight is.' The screech. ' The odd things we share, the sad past.'

Patience Aswa. Patience. Give him some more time.

'I have indeed loved and you must agree with me that a lost love is not an easy topic to discuss.'

She simply nodded. 'When you are searching for love, you are content with dreaming of your desires.' He was deviating. 'When you find love, you are satisfied living with what you've got.' Prose.

'When you lose love..' His voice hushed '- there is an absolute colour lost' Aswa nodded more. A little more patience and she would umpire this interview. Stephen was poised to feed her little stuff and plenty gibbers.

'Love is a raging sea and even in death, it still quakes the soul.' Stephen fixed his eyes on her. 'What do you think, where do we go when we die?' Aswa held his gaze briefly and then rolled her eyes in search of an answer. She didn't need to bother. He continued. 'Do they go the same place when they die naturally and when their lives are just snuffed out?

'Steve, I suppose you are married?' No response. 'In marriage, love is seldom discussed. It's more like action time.'

'Love is an obsession- an obsession crowned in death.' He was stubborn. 'I have had to love and no matter how hard I try to absolve myself, I've had to kill.' He ended in a half scream.

'Steve! Did you say kill?' Her panic was evident. Stephen gave her a reemphasizing glance.

'Like I told you, something just makes me want to open up to you. Perhaps the fact that you are a stranger.'

She swallowed that.

'I don't mean to say that I am your ideal killer but when the wife you love with all your heart dies on your hands and worse still- by your hands, you can't but reappraise who you really are.'

There was a genuine shadow to Stephen's outburst and Aswa could see the valiant fight he was staging against the surging tears.

'Sincerely,' she whispered. ' it's pretty impossible picturing you under that grotesque label.'

'Forget pictures. Forget pictures!' He was palpably agitated. Aswa had a faint feeling that he was mentally deranged. Maybe it came in spurts.

'Julie's body is still in the morgue. These are not the kind of things people joke over.'

She had never thought they were jokes.

'If death came by merit, I assure you she would have lived forever. She was priceless but-' He threw his arms frustratingly to the wind. '-she's gone. Killed by the same hands that swore to protect and love her till eternity.'

Aswa was comprehensively scared now. Spy-wise, it was so far, so good but the tension was starting to build in Stephen's head. She could feel it and she could tell the nearest persons to them was almost seven tables away.

This maniac would her strangled her to death before any help would arrive.

'Please don't get worked up,' she urged him.

'You call that 'work up'?' Stephen dramatically quipped. Aswa trembled inside. This man was unsteady- unpredictable.

Just then, a phone rang. It was Stephen's.

'Hello Lucy.'

Aswa's tripped off. *He even has other women in his life.* She had noted the sudden softness in his voice. *Why wouldn't he kill?* The seconds were passing with difficulty. She had been lucky to sustain this conversation with a mental wreck and she was unwilling to stretch her luck any farther.

She drew her bag close, opened it and returned her hanky. In the same bit, she put off the recorder. Her handbag was a barrel with a ball and socket clip. If Stephen had been as non-gentlemanly as to peep, he would have seen the microcassette recorder.

Stephen muttered a few more incomprehensible words into the phone and hung up. Aswa wasn't interested in what he was sharing with his lover. She was pre-occupied with how she would escape further conversations.

'Once again,' Stephen said pointing at her bag. 'we coincidentally want to leave at the same time. Funny, isn't it?'

'I would rather say strange.'

'Strange then,' Stephen finished.

He offered to drop her off to wherever but she declined. Her excuse was flimsy but at least they exchanged contacts- or so Stephen thought.

Aswa knew that she would be an idiot to feed him with her valid details.

6

4.03 am. Enema sat in front of her house, chewing her tongue to the caressing breeze that usually drew her out. Old habits- for her, never die.

It was her practise back in the years- when life dealt her jabs and blows- to wake up at wee hours and cook *Okpa*- the local food she was renowned for.

Most times, she did it all alone. The mixing of the flour was an art she had perfected over time- having been the daughter of an *okpa* cook. It sounded a little strange to feel that cooking okpa ran in her blood. Well, if it did- she had nipped it. Her Julie was surely never going to cook *Okpa*- commercially, she added. Those days, she would bend over and with her pestle turn and turn the flour, add her warm water, her red oil, *ose*, salt, steer on. She could recollect the details accurately. Why wouldn't she? She had sold *Okpa* to Ikezi people for over 3 decades. It was in the tying that she missed her daughter most. Years ago, when goats and hens were frankly their pets and would often share the same bedroom as they- she always had to wake Julie up once she got to the tying stage. She would dutifully hold the leaves as Enema poured the ready-to-cook delicacy into it. After the exercise, Julie usually returned to finish up her sleep. In that era, the entire family- although just 3 mouths- depended to a huge extent on the proceeds from her wares.

After Julie left the village for further studies abroad, Enema found it a Herculean task having to do it all alone. Once she had made the error of cajoling her husband Otima to assist her in the kitchen and she had almost paid with her livelihood.

She had finished mixing her paste when she excused herself to retrieve the *unere* leaves from the verandah where she customarily allowed early morning dew to touch them. Mirth- nay experience, showed that the spirits added a flavour to the leaves across the night. In her brief exit, her addict of a husband had done his damage.

Perhaps because time changed a whole host of things, she could afford to smile now on reminiscing. It had been anything but funny then. That day she had unsuspectingly carried her ware to the market and it took only a few of her customers facial expression to tell her something was wrong. *Oghe Agu* was more an assemblage of people selling their wares from equidistant poles than it was a market. There were no stalls, no shops, no other structure but very territorial women who knew what exact position belonged to them over the years. The market women never bothered about delineating the market on the basis of the wares sold. But the market thrived- people respected people and almost everyone had an immiscible pool of loyal customers.

On the day in question, Ngevu- the village jester who routinely patronised her, had called her aside to question her.

'If the salt loses its taste, does it turn to snuff?'

Enema was confused. Salt, taste, Snuff. There was a missing link. It was already past midday and by her reputations, her wares were supposed to be almost exhausted by this time. Strangely today was quite slow. Ngevu had prodded her to taste a bit of her own meal.

'Eetiu, Eetiu, Eetiu,' Enema sneezed repeatedly. Just a bite from a piece had sent her nose running. Her eyes glared red and her lungs hurt real bad. The story was just half told. She had been selling poison and didn't realise till now. She glanced across them market to be sure Ngevu had not come as a delegate. If any other person was watching, it wasn't obvious. She quickly but sincerely thanked Ngevu, packed her bag and sped off. It

To Err is Woman

was the first time in twenty years that Enema departed the market with almost all her okpa unsold.

As she walked home, more and more people questioned her wellness. Tears welled up and regressed with each inquiry. Twice, she refused to sell to prospective customers and the moment she caught sight of their hut, the tears broke out. Her integrity had been tarnished grossly.

Otima was a good man. Born with the possibility of becoming wealthy, his father had died most pre-matured and had made the gross error of handing over numerous lands and other assets to his brothers to act as custodians until Otima became of age. At sixty, Otima was yet to come of age in their greedy eyes. They had their own children and as often the case, they successfully dispossessed him of his birth rights. Not being the type to make trouble with kith and kin, he had rid his thoughts of the lewd feelings and concentrated and being able to sustain his wife and eventually his daughter. Fate was not always on his side. He had to give up farming as a source of livelihood when he suddenly woke up with a sprained waist. The hurt was so deep that he had to opt for a job that kept his back straight for most of the day. Bending over was a no no. He had a short stint as a palm-wine tapper- this he also had to give up fast. Eventually he settled into the not so lucrative job of distributing palm wine across homes in the village. Doing that meant that he had to pay the tapper to climb his own palms. It also meant he had to woo people time and time again to patronise his wine. There were also seasons when the entire villagers went on religious streaks of absolute abstinence. Really his market had no pattern unlike his wife's.

Enema was still lying in her tears when her husband strolled in. His penis dangled within the confines of his gown and although it took a trained eye to note that he never wore any pants, it didn't bother him any bit. Fourteen years ago, he had returned home and declared that he was done with wearing any form of pants. Despite Enema's severest persuasions, he really didn't tell her the real reason. Otima realised that he punished himself each time he wore any form of restriction to his ever-sensitive penis. At first, he imagined that it was Enema's presence that aroused him but on close study, he admitted that even the thoughts of his pretty wife provoked an in-surge of blood down there- and he literally thought of her always. As a matter of urgency, he banned under wears and rather wore thicker gowns. As such, he had all-round freedom of expression.

At first glance, he imagined that she sobbed because of the remaining tray-load of *Okpa* he had seen by the door-side.

'Adaugo.' He called her many pet names. ' Don't worry *Nne m. Ha jukwia taa, ha elie ya echi.*'

Though it was the first ever time she was returning home with unsold stock, he knew what obtained amongst other routinely less fortunate okpa sellers. It was an open secret that unsold wares of any day were added to the fresh ones of the next day and they were all sold as '*fresh and hot*'. Of course, unsuspecting customers bought them so.

'Otima, have I not done my bit as your wife?' He was taken aback. 'Have I not loved you as a wife ought to love her man? Must you first ruin my name in Ikeozi before you tell me what I have done to you? Must other women and maidens taunt me to my very face?'

Otima was comprehensively confused. He couldn't tie the outbursts together. He had left home innocuously and he prided himself in having no skeletons in his poor cupboard.

Enema stood up and brought him a piece to eat.

'Eat. Eat,' she encouraged him. 'Eat what you asked me to sell to the entire village.'

Otima boldly took a bite and as he chewed it, his eyes opened like Adam's.

Shame spontaneously replaced surprise and although Enema saw the transformation, she didn't relent with her lamentations.

That day had changed a lot of things about them. They were a couple that stayed close, perhaps because they had little by means of possession and children but after that incident, they had become more closely knit together.

In a way, Enema was glad Otima had made that mistake. The scandal had lasted just one season. The Ikeozi cultural group had made a song of the woman who sold what she couldn't stand.

Ada Ikeozi. I-na eresi onye?
Nri o bu nri oha?
oha nke I na esoro?
Onye rie o na-achi.
Irie, gi na azuzu a na-eme…

No names were mentioned but the tongue always could count the teeth. Most importantly, Otima had placed a seal on tobacco *'utaba'* and for just that, Enema loved him deeper.

Today, Enema shut her eyes briefly and thanked Obasi. It had been prophetic when her mother- at first glance had named her daughter- Nwakaego. She eventually grew up as Julie especially when as she said 'the white folks were mutilating her name'. Julie was her only child and she really didn't wish for any more. She bore the household with a capability three sons would have found difficult to match. In one clean swipe, Julie had erased every item in the house. The old had quickly made way for the new. Without much bidding, Julie possessed her thoughts as well. Julie had in little less than a year erected them a stupendous mansion and in spite of her persistent worry about the exaggerated number of rooms, her daughter had calmly assured her that someday each of the eight rooms would be occupied. That was another prophesy she impulsively clung to. She was worried that so far, Julie had only bore Zwitt. In her wildest fantasies, she anticipated five more.

Enema opened her eyes. She could hear some rustling of cashew tree leaves. Did they ever cease to rustle? The hens were starting to wake up. She could decipher voices coming towards the house. They were still a safe distance away but their calm voice travelled in the quietness of the dark. Enema was genuinely frightened; in all her years of routine wake-ups, such incidents were usually reactionary. Uncommon things occur for uncommon reasons. At the edge of the house, the voices froze. They either had said all they willed or they had perceived her presence. Nothing unnerved Enema more than uncertainty.

Suddenly a feminine laughter roared into the docile dawn. Enema could have sworn that there had been just two men until the piercing sounds sunk into her ears. The reverberations seemed to have transformed into words. They had never gone mute- they had only tampered their voices further.

'What do you know?' The tones rose a little. They were repeating that phrase way too often. The words seemed to echo in her head now. Indeed, she knew she knew nothing. To know, she sprouted up and tiptoed to where the voices came from. Per chance, she could draw close enough to inquire what it was that had happened or better still- eavesdrop.

She was convinced something had happened in Ikeozi. Her instincts guaranteed her it was something bad.

As she approached, she listened carefully.

'Even flying eggs lay their birds on the ground,' a male voice said. 'Don't they know the air is safer?'

Enema was sure he meant flying birds.

'Who are we to say what should happen where?' the other asked.

'Who we are?' the lady enthused. 'We are the three mad ones of Ikeozi.' She followed it up with another outburst of laughter and again the echo taunted Enema.

'What do you know?'

At that point, Enema could have turned back. At least she knew the Ikeozi mad three- Mpufe, Adichi and Moe. Household names they were. Reputable mad souls of Ikeozi. Still, there was something odd about this meeting.

As far as Ikeozi's history went, the three had never seen eye to eye on any issue at any time. There was a grand controversy which had climaxed when both had begun to make simultaneous overtures at Mpufe. Both mad men wanted to have her for keeps- the height of territoriality. She too had her own price; anyone who wanted her must stoop to her 'classical' intelligence and overt cognitive abilities. Her ambition was to become 'Baba ndi ala- the Supreme Leader of the Mad Gang'. No matter, how insane both men were, they wouldn't settle for a woman leader. On that note they agreed but they repeatedly tried treacherous means to get her to become branded by one of them. The triangle of covetousness hardly ever allowed the trio a non-incidental moment of encounter. They taunted one another, the men would make mock fights and move on. Mpufe too used her appeal to the utmost with intermittent flings with any of the two but never the two at once.

To have the trio holding a polite conversation at the foot of her home was very eerie.

Enema wasn't sure what to do next. She just leaned on a little closer.

'Adaugo,' Otima called from a couple of yards behind.

In a flash, the three were gone. Enema stood still for a moment, disappointed and worried.

It would have pacified her to hear more of the even gibberish talk and their sudden flight didn't dissipate her fright.

She returned to her even more worried husband. He too had even strangely woken up a little earlier and had been alarmed to see his wife perched at a corner of the house. As far as his eyes could stretch, there were no other persons in sight. All houses in the village were unfenced except the Chief's.

Enema gulped in some air and steadied her neurons.
Let the day break.

Lucy wound her glasses down and spat into road. Nothing stimulated her gustatory centres like the sight of dirt. All through the journey she had been repeating the feat- spitting into the filth and wondering what the league of people who said Lagos was grimy had seen before they drew their conclusions. Sedentary senile bastards. They probably hadn't gone past Ore-Benin road. The roads were littered by mind-bogging waste.

She had undertaken this journey without a pre-notification of either her would-be hosts nor a permission from her husband. She had persistently consulted on herself as she drove. The initial doubts she entertained as to whether she could pull off the long distance drive from Lagos to Delta were shaken off the first time she overtook another lady driver. The many times they had travelled to the village, it was always her husband that drove. The only time she dared to man the wheels, he had quickly taken over before they could do a kilometre. It was a man's world. Or it used to be…until Julie drove herself once to join them in the village. Lucy had been hugely inspired. In fact, she opined that she could drive beyond Ikeozi into Amazim- just to go further than her rival. *She's dead*, she reminded herself. The competition was over and won. *Was it*?

She had patiently waited for Stephen to leave for work before she began any bit of her preparation. From her scheduling, she would return before he did- all things being equal. Not that it mattered if she returned later or never. She had plenty of lies in stock. Lucy had ordered Zwitt to get ready and asked George to prepare himself for a little trip. Geria didn't take much of her time.

None of the three kids knew where they were headed to but the excitement of a sudden journey was resplendent on both George and Geria. Zwitt was simply passive, obeying instructions and awaiting further orders. They had all worn clearly outstanding clothes- routine for all but Zwitt. Lucy never thought of how unbearably long five hours could be but after two hours on the trail, she wished she had planned for it.

The Kia baby jeep's stereo set was damaged- an electrical fault that she could have quickly fixed if she had pulled over for twenty minutes at any radio electricians. She rued that hurry as she had to endure the scorching silence once Geria and George had exhausted their pendulous chatters and fallen asleep. What pained her most was the shudder she felt every time she caught Zwitt's eyes through the rear-view mirror.

After the first three eye bumps, she had instructed Zwitt to switch positions with Geria. Her daughter's eyes were shut but at least her face was friendlier. Sadly, the strategy didn't work, her gaze kept chasing Zwitt. She couldn't get used to it- no matter how often they locked.

Lucy forced her attention to the streets.

They had met an ongoing reconstruction work around Ore and alongside other commuters they had had to take a diversion that found them mingling through the ancient streets of Ondo state. Of course she didn't know the sub-route but she boldly followed the traffic. It was amazing how many decades it was taking the federal government to do this road. In fact, recent myth had it that the youths of Ore town engaged in nocturnal destruction of the roads at every given opportunity. Their inspiration wasn't ambiguous; they needed the traffic jams to fuel their economy. An economy that revolved around hawking and robbery- their own dividends of democracy. Lucy stayed in queue making sure the presumably east-bound Peace Mass Transit bus never disappeared from her view. After about an hour of meandering within the village, the bus suddenly pulled up. Lucy marched her brakes abruptly, her nerves starting to tremble. What the heck was wrong with this driver?

The driver opened his door and started to walk towards her car. She was confused. Had she been led into a trap? With a quick snap, she got all the doors pinned.

The man approached her end of the car and knocked on her glass. Lucy observed him. He didn't look dangerous and there were no uneven bulges on his clothes.

'Madam, wetin?' She read his lips.

Again the man knocked on the glass. Lucy took in the surrounding. Fewer cars were plying this route compared to the streams of cars that had

Obiora Oji

obviously been diverted off the express. The driver had definitely led her off the main road.

She braved it and wound down, then made a 'what is it' face.

'Wetin make you de follow me up and down?' He had withdrawn the courteous Madam.

'Follow you ke- as in?'

The driver had one way or the other noticed that Lucy's car had blindly tailed him and for confirmatory purposes, he had deviated and she had stupidly followed. However the tint on her glasses had not allowed him decipher the occupants of the vehicle. He wouldn't have worried if he had known they were just a lady and a couple of kids. It was a brave effort on his own part to pull up and accost whoever was stalking his car.

Anyway, if he had expected a subtle plea for guidance from this woman, he was in for rude one.

'Na you be main road abi na you be Julius Berger?' Lucy was already remonstrating. The man was stunned.

'Abeg, i take God beg u..no follow me again, abeg!' He said finally. He was not in the mood to bicker with a woman. Not when his passengers were waiting and he had to book a turn at the company's pit if he arrived early. He turned and walked back to his bus.

Lucy sighed loudly. George had woken up with the screech of her tyres but the omni-present Zwitt was the one who understood what had just gone down. They were lost and without a compass. She allowed the bus speed off before she killed her engine and took in deeper than deep breaths. She had to ask the locals or risk trying to trace her way back. After a couple of minutes, she drove off-slowly and observably. At last, she saw her chance. A fast food spot- not amorously decorated but she could use what she had to get the answers she needed. She had cash. Just before she alighted, she took her kids orders. George and Geria wanted ice cream and meat-pies. Lucy had meticulously asked them by their names.

Zwitt wasn't asked so he didn't profer. Lucy quickly returned with double treats for George and Geria.

'You can have this,' she said offering Zwitt a thin doughnut and a warm satchet of pure water as she climbed back into the steering.

Zwitt muttered a thank you and slowly began to eat. Lucy kept her chocolates on the vacant front seat and from there, she fetched them at will. She knew it was a matter of time before Geria would demand for chocolate. From the edge of her rear-view mirror, she delightfully peeped at Zwitt as he gnawed at the hole in the dough.

It was almost three hours since they left home and the meal was re-vitalising. Five minutes after the snacks, Lucy reduced the air-condition to confirm what sounds were being blown into her ears.

True to her fears, it was Zwitt singing.

This was the first time since Juliet passed on that she was hearing him speak so many words. He was actually singing more words than he had totalled all these months.

His clear-cut almost baritone voice rang through the box of a jeep. The lyrics flowed with an accent of authority as though the song was designed to minister to someone. Lucy struggled to catch his gaze but he had turned his face to squarely stare at Geria. It even appeared his eyes were shut to the sight of his siblings relishing in the taste of their ice creams.

'My mommy is over the ocean..my mommy is over the sea-'

The phrases flung into Lucy's ears. She could barely tame her concentration to stay on the road. Before this recital, the song was once of her few ever-greens, it reminded her of the spurts of affections she shared with her mother. It always had a soothing effect on the sores in her heart.

That was then. Anger thumped at her heart. The lullaby was coming from the wrong lips and even if the voice was as classical as Jim Reeve's, she couldn't take it any second longer. In that instant, Zwitt's voice froze as though knowingly.

Lucy sneered and waited. She would have quelled the song forever in her own unique pattern.

She peeped at Zwitt again. George was telling him something in regrettably inaudible tones. Lucy sniffed and drove on.

Sharper, louder and more intrusive than before, the song-turned chant resumed. It eroded her ears- the combination of Zwitt's calm tone and George's perforated voice. Lucy was larger than disgusted.

She jammed the brakes and the song was obliterated by the sudden halt. She made a u-turn to face both boys- the fury jumping out from her eyes.

'George,' she said from in between her teeth. 'don't be an idiot.'

Both boys were still confused. George couldn't stand the fury in her eyes. He focused on her necklace instead. That equally annoyed Lucy.

'So if this animal says his mother has been flung into River Niger, you also will follow him and sing?'

She said the flung with a sneer.

Coincidentally, Lucy had pulled over beside the river. The aura of the water aided her communication.

George thought over the mother's question. He could do anything to avert her temper.

He rigorously shook his head.

Lucy allowed a 'now listen very well' silence to pass as her eyes roamed from the three kids to the river by the road. In a flash, she considered actually throwing Zwitt into the waters and ending his life of awaiting miseries. She could pull off the stunt and go scot free but something strangely assured her that he would swim to safety.

'Bad mothers abandon their kids,' she started. 'But good mothers always stay around.'

Zwitt read the underlying message perfectly. He refused to as much as wink.

Lucy was not satisfied. She craved for a stinger.

'And bad mothers always end up in Hell, smelling Satan's bum-bum' she added.

The boy was damn too predictable. A barrage of sad tears poured down his cheeks. Soft pumpkin, she thought.

Zwitt felt the warmth of the tears as they poured on his chest. It hurt him to imagine his dear mother being tormented in hell. He knew about the fire- she herself had told him stories of how gruesome Hell was. If Lucy had spoken factually, then Zwitt had plenty reasons to weep for Mama.

Lucy scowled and ingeniously hummed a tune. It was an instant hit.

'Zwitt's mama- in hell..serving Satan- in hell.'

With a trio of urging nods, George quickly picked up the chorus.

Lucy turned on the ignition. Who needed radios anymore? The anthem was simple, straight and efficient.

7

It was well past midday and the scorching sun was making it impossible for everyone. Enema and Otima sat under the six year old orange tree and from its shade, they supervised the three labourers who frantically attacking the soil in a rush to leave the intense sun. Their raffia hats did next to nothing in providing the, any succour.

Enema lifted her eyes and counted the oranges within view. It was the plants first productive season and though they had anticipated its fruitfulness to start about three years back, she was still happy the tree eventually began. The much-talked about 'Agric' seeds seemed to have difficulties living up to expectation on this particular soil. She bought them- about six little plants at fairly costly prices and it had just been this one that stood the harmattan when it arrived. Of course, she had routinely watered all of them but the other five had chosen to whither- much to her dismay. In any case, she had kept faith with this one and reaping was imminent.

A recallable number of years ago, it would have been the couple- insensitively and passionately toiling for the fruits of the ground. In those days, gender made very little difference as they usually shared out the marked-out portion between them. Otima somehow got a slightly larger area but hours of fierce tilling saw them finishing at about the same time.

A smile swept across Enema's face as she recollected some of the battles she had had to fight just to stay alive. Very often, with her back bent to the ground, she pondered on what profitable venture she would engage in next. The ends just had to meet. That was her mandate. No strife was too much as long as they didn't starve.

Now, her direst worry was how to stay ordinary in the eyes of villagers. She reminded herself of the ancient tale of the low-life girl who had by some stroke of divine fortune, become the wife of a king. The orphan had made a dramatic turn-around in attitude. Her humility which had indeed earned her such unprecedented status quickly turned to sheer arrogance and irrepressible pride. Agbomma- as the story had it quickly shed all her maiden names and assumed very alien names which even the pronunciation laid emphasis on how 'levels had changed'. Her old-time mates were not spared the brunt of her intimidation. No-one had exclusive right of entry to her presence. No-one shared right of passage with her when she visited the markets.

Many of her peers had words they wished they could share with her. Words that had first crept around as gossip and would have helped her preserve her throne.

Things did change fast, especially where caution is misspelled as 'cushion'. Within two barren years of marriage, the young king had silently noticed the aggression which hallmarked his wife's ascent to power. If he complained to anyone- it wasn't the Queen or Ekerutimeia- as she would insist she be called. Wherever she adopted the name from, the story never explained.

However the story stated that when Agbomma's cup ran over, the king had unceremoniously deposed her and quickly replaced her with a brand new wife.

The rest was easy to imagine.

Aka ekpuchi onwa. That was the simple answer to Enema dutiful battle to mask the wealth that Julie had bestowed upon them. She made constant efforts to reach out to some of her less fortunate peers. Her situation was an innate pointer that the world really turns around. Her beneficiaries were if not for anything- inspired by the fact that poverty-struck Enema of yesterday could really put food on their tables. *O te aka odiwalu njo, o di mma.* They were constantly reminded by her story that there was hope for tomorrow.

Consequent to a wardrobe overhaul, neither Otima nor Enema had what could be classically described as a 'farm' cloth.

Enema wore her brown linen wrapper today against a transparent while blouse. Her dark brassieres were strapped across her bust. She was probably the only Ikeozi woman who owned a handless bra and she could wear hers to the farm!

An unexpected breeze delightfully waved the neat lock of her hair across her face and in her peculiar romantic style, she returned the hair to their status quo.

There is a drop of romance in every woman. Enema didn't need to attend a love course to learn the feminine swag. She put her head on Otima's shoulder and giggled straight into the right ears. The sun could shine all it wanted, she had no qualms with openly displaying her affection for him anywhere., Their body language unmistakeably suggested that love was burning them up.

'That corner,' Otima said pointing at one of the farmers at the extreme. 'It should be reserved for only cassava. That soil hasn't been good on maize-ever.'

'I thought that was the area you promised Efeani,'

Otima in recollection. Efeanidi was the once upon a time best hunter in the village. Most bush meat in the market had his trademark- single shot fatal bullets or tiny indentations from his customized arrows or traps. His reputation of course dwarfed the modest efforts of the rest of the league of Ikeozi hunters. There were no outright show of envy nor any premonition of bad days to come for him. It was a shock when the village woke up to the thick smoke that filled the whole skies. Efeanidi's hunting space had been razed down by a mysterious fire. As though that development wasn't shocking enough, the renowned hunter had woken up the next day paralyzed on one side. Of course, tongues wagged. It was strange that there was no particular suspect. Efeanidi seemed to have co-existed in peace with everyone who crossed his way. His exploits were celebrated and even revered by the younger generation. He was a legend and won bragging rights to the neighbouring villages. It was unthinkable that such evil should befall such a man. When it seemed like there were no human suspects, people deviated to the supernatural. Some soft story about how the Meat-hunter had been accosted by a deer a fortnight before the misfortune. The deer was reported to have spoken to him. Not spoken but warned him to desist from preying on her kind. He was mandated to never step his foot on the hunting ground- if he loved his life. Being the courageous son of his father- he had of course flaunted the entreaty. In the days following the disaster, he could hardly talk and some measure of saliva drooled off the side of his deviated mouth. At a point, people had written him off as mad. He had probably shot the god's animal or eaten some forbidden fruit. It took him some months to considerably recover some strength in his limbs and as his sovereign status vanished, he resorted to alms from a few enlightened ones to feed. The rest wouldn't be part of it- assisting him whom the gods had cursed. The educated ones fairly understood a thing or two about raised blood pressure and the effect of stress. But there was hardly a forum to educate the other ones.

'We shall have to give him a more fertile portion,' Otima suggested. 'Whatever he wishes to grow will do well at Ndida.' The latter was a valley-like mass of land that always churned out plantains and banana-heads in quantum. It was a choice area.

Enema glanced up at him and then transforming her thoughts into words, she complimented him, 'Ezigbo di di mma.'

Otima glowed. Her suggestions were never less than perfect. The woman he married hadn't changed much after over three decades. The warmth had neither waned nor did the care and confidence she lavished on him ebb. The round unwrinkled face, dark searching eyes constituted an irrepressible clutch on his heart. She was the one with the sole license to sing his worries away and even more mysteriously drown her own disappointments.

Their union was a love song on perpetual repeat.

'I don't think it would be wise for us to return home together,' she began. 'And there would be no lunch for any of us.' Otima nodded and in that bid, some water missed his gaping mouth and splashed across his jaw unto her face.

He paused. 'I'll watch them conclude the remaining ridges. You can trot home.'

Enema counted out the wages and handed them over to her husband. Another hiatus Julie's absence had created. If their daughter was around, she would have merrily offered to go make food for the farm-folks. Julie hated farm-life. In her second post-pubertal farming season, she found a strange effrontery and had voiced out her disgust for the mud and dirt. That day, the trio had come in the evening to disseminate the fresh manure that had been dumped on their land. Julie had suddenly started to sniff and make faces that suggested outright repulsion for the heap of maggots and offensive smell. Otima had in the first ten minutes of their stay ignored his daughter while Enema cautioned her with her eyes. It was a little strange that Julie didn't heed the silent motherly warnings on the evening.

'Ego, you can go,' Otima stated from out of the blues. Enema had been surprised. She knew Otima only called their daughter Ego when he was pissed. For the young girl, there was no room for discernment. The offer was good; an early dismissal from the 'nyama nyama'. She turned to go and even Enema's sceptical eyes were not prepared for what followed. Otima rained balls of wet manure at her daughter. Julie ran in comical circles, trailed by very accurate throws from her dad until she hid behind her mum- her body splashed with the same 'nyama nyama'. Thirty minutes later, her screams and sobs had evaporated to a silent obedient girl carrying about her expected duties.

Men had their ways.

'See you later,' she called out after rendering her peck.

After nearly ten minutes of knocking, Zwitt returned to the car. He wished he didn't have to deliver the obvious news to Lucy. His tired legs were threatening to buckle but he kept spirit.

'There's nobody at home- Ma.' A throat-full of saliva swam down.

'Idiot, you don't call me Ma,' Lucy screamed. She pushed her head out of the window and closer to his ears. 'You say Mommy. Do you understand?'

Zwitt nodded until Lucy almost asked him to stop. He was over-understanding.

Lucy studied the host of half-naked small village folks that had escorted her car from the junction through the uneven road surface up to the house. A couple of the boys had their plastic balls in their hands- they had apparently abandoned their football matches to do the mini-marathon with her car. The stern smile-free scrutiny drove their excitement away, one after another.

Lucy was certain they had never seen a meaner face. The little crowd vanished- scurrying away as though their lives were in danger. It was common practise to run after foreign vehicles, direct them if the drivers were confused and be appreciated with cash or often- a pack of cabin biscuits.

'Scary thing,' she taunted Zwitt. 'See how you have driven your friends away.'

Zwitt nodded albeit stupidly. She could see that he was exhausted but she had that urge to leave him standing off the vehicle for a little longer.

'Zwitt, come in now,' Geria pleaded. She could have read her mother's mind.

Zwitt didn't move a muscle. Experience had taught him who gave the last order. He smiled weakly at her and kept his ground.

'Didn't you hear her? Eeh?' she howled.

As he climbed back, he admitted to himself that there was indeed no hard and fast rules about whom to obey. If he acted on Geria's words on another day- it would entail outright crucifixion from her mother. He just had to stay sensitive to the delicate art of slavery.

Lucy knew why she let Geria override her wishes. Julie's parents had to be quarantined against noticing any show of bias as she narrated her innocent tale.

She had travelled all those miles to instigate a deep cry for vengeance. It was somehow good neither Otima nor Enema was at home yet. At least she had the chance to tie up her story. It was a visit that required cautious dressing and she had won her dull grey aso-oke- a rare apparel preserved for funerals or very moody outings- like today. Anyone who knew her trend of clothing would raise an eyebrow at her choice today but that was the motive- raise eyebrows, 'nosebrows'- everything arousable. Her hair was scuffled across her head as though she had endured a rain-flog and then had an hasty sun burn.

There were no stick on the lips, no perfumes and no jewelleries. She needed to impress upon them the image of a woman who had packed her kids and fled in fright. Her appearance would speak even before she uttered a word.

'Ikuozu, Ikuozu,' George was insisting. The loser's frown was creeping into his face.

'It's Ikeozi, George,' Zwitt corrected him glancing his smart eyues around for a proof- signposts or home addresses. In Lagos, such arguments died before they could even be called an argument as there were pointers and indicators everywhere. On this occasion, he saw none. 'Am sure it's Ikeozi,' he firmly added.

George took the best- ever available option. Even if he hadn't, Lucy would have still stepped in.

'Mommy, is it Ikuoza or-' He couldn't even produce the other. George hardly knew anything completely. Even his 'Ikuozu' had transformed to 'Ikuoza'.

'It's Ikuoza dear,' Lucy confirmed.

'I thought-' Lucy's petrifying stare shrugged off every doubt.

'Ikuoza, Ikuoza,' Zwitt repeated.

Good for you, sharp brain my foot. Though the lessons were endless, she wasn't convinced that Zwitt was latching up well. If he was, he wouldn't dare argue with her kids or her- for that matter.

'Mommy can we go play on the sand,' Geria asked politely.

'No,' Lucy whispered 'You can go,' she finished as she thought better of it. Spontaneity of reversals were not very new anymore. First and foremost, because the request came from Geria, it was unthinkable that she could decline it in front of this little idiot. Secondly, an unsupervised feel of sand would help grow some gel between the kids quickly. Lastly, she needed some quiet time right now.

The rear door opened and they hopped into the white sand.

Lucy relaxed into her seat, unbuckling her seat belt in the process. She heard some movement right behind her.

She could have sworn that she was alone.

'What are you doing here?' she shrieked at Zwitt.

He kept mute.

'Common go and join them,' she commanded.

Zwitt quietly crept out. Lucy was pleased that he had learnt how to exclude himself from the 'we' her children often said.

Who said the young lad wasn't learning?

Otima quietly walked through the bush paths, his water jug firmly strapped across his shoulder. Though he strode without visible anxiety, he prayed that his house would come into view- and the prayers became more earnest with each turn. The supplications of a bold fronted very hungry man.

His leather sandals were heavier than usual and he absent-mindedly wished he was still in the era of wearing his bare-foots to the farm. Some of these civil things Julie had forced down his throat were outright inconveniences. This was a path he had walked for as many years as he didn't bother to remember and it was unthinkable for him not to know where to put his feet. He knew the alignment of the stones, the composition of the soil and where the grasses had bristles. Without these extra loads on his feet, he was certain he would get home faster and unharmed except of course the gods remembered him unkindly. Just the way they had visited Efeanidi. He shrugged off the idea as he bent forward to remove the sandals. He was not really a fetish figure. His father had been one of the first few Ikeozians that embraced the white man's religion. A hypocritical embrace it had seemed because at every gray area, the man had always stuck with his native doctrines. He was a hybrid Christian- borrowing principles from each religion as they would favour his cause.

Early African Christians were not different from the present generation. Infact they had laid the template of ambiguity that often undermined the essence of their Christianity. Hard-core issues like the Osu-caste system was a controversial issue; as much as they preached their 'born-againism' and oneness in Christ, they quickly reneged on all entreaties once any of theirs showed hints of mingling with any outcastes. It didn't help the cause of the religion- at least locally. The obstinate off-shoot of these pioneer Christians who had acted upon their 'strange' faith were quickly ostracized and declared unclean.

So, Otima was on track in his worry. If the gods were truly after Efeanidi, he would be invoking their anger by offering any form of assistance. Any substantial assistance, he corrected himself. Enema had already taken food to him on many occasions- not to talk of the money he had personally given him. How was he to know?

Otima was not a very endearing person in the village- most of the friction stemmed out of the fact that he spoke rarely and never made a conscious effort to amuse anyone. He just held his own. He frankly didn't think that he had any living enemies within the village unless of course his changing status had attracted a couple of jealous eyes. Why would it? While he was poor, he had been poor by himself. He had neatly arranged his life even in that low-class; family first, belief next and any other could trail.

Anyone who despised that order had better stay off.

His peripatetic senses perceived some ukwa scent from somewhere. He prayed the aura wasn't false- although breadfruit was the last meal he expected Enema to prepare.

Surprises were not new with his wife though.

'Your heart is ahead of your feet.'

Otima spurned around fiercely. He didn't notice anyone follow him this closely behind. Besides, this route was known to very few foot soldiers.

Ekwenta laughed victoriously- delighted with the transient panic his tiny frame had evoked. Otima relaxed on identifying him. It was unusual that he hadn't noticed him sitting at the foot of the tree even though he had glanced cursorily at the tree some seconds earlier.

'Ekwe- where did you come out from?' Otima half-laughed back. 'You weren't there just now.'

Again Ekwenta roared in hearty laughter. Who could have thought that he too could appear and vanish.

'You keep your mind where your treasure lies, Otima.'

He stared into his face. 'Is your treasure at the foot of Ukwu-ugba?' Ekwenta didn't answer.

'True talk,' Otima conceded. It was pointless debating when he was this farmished. 'I have a home and a wife to run home to but-,' he hesitated. 'I still don't believe you were there and I could pick you out.'

He tactically didn't mention the food he was fleeing to. Ikeozi men could be funny attimes-they would suddenly tag alongside you once they knew your meal was waiting- unapologetically.

'A man calls unto the things that are before him. You may know that I am a small man but to remind me is mockery.'

Dwarfs were notably short fused and very eager to display their tempers.

'My friend, my eyes had indeed gone with my heart.' Otima added. 'Please forgive me.'

Ekwenta nodded consent. 'Otima,' he began. His tone was sobered- a erratic deviation from himself. 'So many men have homes and so many homes have wives in them'

Otima listened patiently. The hunger had waned for curiosity.

'Our fathers taught us that as we make our beds so shall we lie on them,' he continued. Otima nodded. 'But they deceived us.' Ekwenta was flaring up again. 'So many men have made their beds and gone to the farm, only to return to a rumpled one later in the day.' He chewed his teeth loudly.

'Our ancestors omitted something,' he declared. Otima wondered what it was. Ekwenta was notorious for verbosity but not with parables and tongue-twisters.

'When you wish to lie on a made bed, stand around it. Don't go anywhere,' he literally warned.

There was little sense- frankly much sense, in his conclusion but the relevance of the topic was not striking.

'Does your daughter drive a boat?'

Ekwenta was getting personal. Family first, Otima cautioned himself. However he gave him the benefit of his curiosity and shook his head.

'I saw a boat of tears rowing towards your house.'

Otima was disappointed with himself. He had waved his hunger aside to listen attentively to this pervert. A drunk's evening exercise.

Ekwenta laughed bitterly this time; Otima was worried his thoughts translated to his face but at this point, he cared less.

'Go, before the boat drowns the sea.' He declared. 'Go before the bed has no one to lie on it.'

Otima required no further dismissal. He nodded and half-ran- away from Ekwenta and his riddles.

The wailing was gradually dying down although Enema sobbed discontinuously. The sitting room was in total disarray, people sat in random mournful litters grunting and speaking in hushed tones. In between moments, there were waves of silence that allowed everyone pursue his independent thoughts. Within the room, every mind flew in wild directions.

Lucy's arms were roped around Enema who in turn held Zwitt to her chest. Otima sat transfixed and abruptly pale at the corner of the house- surrounded by three men. His eyes were avidly open but everybody knew he wasn't there with them. Once in a while, voices penetrated his thoughts with 'Ndo nu'. Condolences.

'Julie mo, Julie, ofu anya ji isi ugwo,' Enema sang painfully. Lucy rocked her soothingly. She too had tears strolling down her face. Nature itself was collaborating her scheme. Breaking the news first-hand to Enema had been an instant success. It was only a doting mother who could pick the panic she bore from her face. Only a mother with an extremely high index of suspicion would worry over her returning home with the kids, without Julie.

Lucy had laboriously played the competent bad tale bearer but it only took two nervous inquiries from Enema to break her down.

'What? Which Julie?' Enema could barely hear herself. She flung her head-gear away and launched for Lucy. She was a master dramatist, Lucy thought as her pre-prepared tears flooded her eyes.

'Ewoo Chi mo!' Enema's cry pierced the clouds. Lucy attempted to bring her close but she had gone mad with grief. She shoved her aside and ran away from her house wailing at the top of her voice.

Lucy resisted the temptation to pursue her but silently hoped Enema didn't go any extra hurtful mile. She was way too tired to race after a grief-struck woman.

Suddenly the wails retraced back to the house. She smiled herself. Enema must have been disenchanted by Julie's reluctance to run after her- as was traditional in Ikeozi. Lucy sat still and wept loudly. None of her kids were in sight and that was good for the game.

However Enema's return wasn't quite spontaneous. She had been headed for the river- Ekwi and now as she was led back by the two women who had intercepted her bid. If she hadn't been wailing at top voice, she would have successfully gotten to Ekwi. The rest would have been history but at least she would have saved herself this agony. But how could she not cry? At the death of her only daughter? Her son equivalent? Her only child? Her everything?

She wasn't going to live through it, she told herself. They could guard and watch over her for the day but she was sure she would get her chance. She was billed to join her daughter.

Lucy had glanced up to inspect the little crowd that shepherded Enema home. The rest of the beans had to be shelved- at least till Otima showed face.

'My God, what have i done?' Enema quizzed, looking up to the ceiling. What had God done to her? She paid her tithes- punctually for that matter, gave freewill donations and daily implored God to protect Julie. Yet! How could God be this mean? He could have let her stay barren, the way she had come to the world than give her this high dose of pain. He could have taken her instead and left her charming Julie alone. He could have taken the both of them at once.

Her eyes moved to where Otima sat. Three of them at once in fact. Did

God truly exist? Of course he did. She had prayed for a child and gotten Julie. Who then prayed for this calamity? Where had she missed it and God was punishing her in severe ways. It was unthinkable that Nwakaego was gone. The joy and cheer she gave them was snatched away without a warning. No! She was going to follow!

The gathering pool of tears from Zwitt were stuck on Enema's forearm. She felt something cold and realized she had tightly clutched Zwitt's neck. She slackened her grip and the pool dissipated.

Otima's eyes were still wide open. The horrific image of his smiling Julie lying in her own blood surfaced with every blink of his eyes. He couldn't dare shutting them. How the mighty had fallen. His scurry from Ekwenta had turned to a full race when he heard wails emanating from his house. The scent of the breadfruit had vanished and even now, he had no idea at what spot he flung his sandals and water jug away.

He had run home, hyper-alert and prepared for the worst until he heard. Only then did he realize that he wasn't prepared at all.

Otima had slumped into the sands and seconds later when he sat up, he just cried like a baby.

Few people bothered to console him.

Men don't cry, they say. But when you see a man shedding tears, you had better let it be.

Lucy knew the drill. She let him cry for a while and then requested to speak to him in private. She didn't have all day to break all of the news and a tiring journey lay ahead for her.

Since the end of that conversation, Otima had just stood at the corner of the home where Lucy had led him. Tears had dried from his eyes and his face was masked with vengeful bitterness.

His brief dialogue- or was it briefing with Lucy replayed in his mind.

'Daddy,' Lucy sobbed. 'Stephen knows what, Stephen knows what happened to Julie. There was no mistake.' She blew her nose into her handkerchief and made no effort to wipe the tears.

'We were all there,' she continued.

Otima was lost in thoughts. This was an unexpected twist. It was bad enough that Julie had been killed.

'Otherwise after so many days,' Lucy continued. 'You would have thought that he would have come home himself- to inform you.' Lucy had at that point turned to the wall for support.

'If he finds out that I have been here, he's surely going to kill me too,' she lamented.

''He won't find out,' Otima had reassured her. Words were deserting him. 'He won't find out,' he repeated. He just couldn't think out something else.

'After some hard earned advices from each other, they had returned to the sitting- 'wailing' room.

Stephen. Stephen. Stephen. Where is thy sting? Otima was wounded in his spirit.

8

Three consecutive attempts to stir up Lucy's libido saw both lovers at opposite ends of the bed. It was a generously sized bed and it took twelve full roll overs to reach one end from the other. Despite its size, it was one that had endured very lonely seasons recently. It's overhead lamps were hardly used and it appeared no-one remembered its in-built stereo; another of his under-used assets.

When Stephen had found Lucy lying at the centre of his bed, he was genuinely surprised. He was an expressive man and in spite of the tragic moments, he still had urges at sporadic moments. Like the lady at forever had almost induced. He mechanically suppressed the stray emotions pending the completion of the funeral rites. It was imaginably going to be quite a break but his wife had appeared in her filmy night gown, erotically poised on his bed. Her choice of the centre of the bed said the rest. She wanted something. Stephen's meagre resolve was deleted in a flash. Lucy was human, he had reasoned. It was not justifiable punishing the living for the dead. They could enjoy this singular occasion- in loving memory of his honey- Julie. He was quickly proved wrong.

As he held his own lines, his hands greedily clasped round one of the fat pillows. He struggled to solve the mystery that his Lucy had become. Had he changed or everyone else had changed towards him. Things were no longer what they appeared. Really, things no longer appeared.

He had a brain-load of worries on his head and no-one to share them with and as he pressed the pillow firmer on his chest, he wished he hadn't gone headlong to make false assumptions. Not this night. Where hadn't his mind gone to, in anticipated ecstasy.

The night was a cold one and even the stone-cold Lucy felt it. She had neatly tucked herself under the blankets and stayed prone. Stephen was sure she was thinking as well.

He waited for his erection to subside. It wasn't seeming imminent. That was his biggest sexual challenge. Once he was aroused, even a court injunction could dispel it. He shut his eyes and bit his lips. His rigid penis pushed at his boxers relentlessly. He wondered what he could do next. If he removed the boxers, the trapped animal would be jubilant. So also would his tormentor. He decided against it, instead he turned to back her.

Lucy attended to Stephen's disappointed body movements. He lay a handsome distance away but the hot heavy breaths resonated across the bedroom.

She was sure she had him. Time ebbed away and his breaths stayed hot and hungry. He was undeniably in the mood. She had waved off his earlier gestures to confirm how deep his desires were. Knowing his sexual profile, she doubted that he could do these few weeks without making love and since she hadn't been approached for such pleasures, she feared that he was getting serviced outside. Her fears were needless.

Ten roll-overs and she lay beside him. His body was nervously rigid at her first touch.

'Stephen dear,' she began as her fingers ran through his hair down to his ears. He hadn't shaved since Julie passed on. 'I know it's not going to be easy for us considering what our family has passed through and is passing through.' She paused as Stephen turned to face her.

'I truly want to be the best wife you can ever have.'

Stephen looked serious. 'Not as a replacement to Julieee-.' She was finding weeping all the more easy with every stunt. '-because I know she way beyond special to us,'

'I want to be the best wife as myself-Lucy.'

Stephen could not believe his ears. He held Lucy's face and felt the tears on her cheeks.

'The pain is just hard to erase but together-,' His voice broke. ' we can march on.'

Both pulled close to each other, under the warmth of their tears and the cover of the blanket. Some time passed as though they were wondering on who to press what buttons to press first.

'There's someone who's hurting more than all of us,' Lucy whispered into his ears.

'Who?' He searched her face. The tears were not there anymore.

'Zwitt' Lucy answered solemnly. 'Stephen that boy has a soft spot for his mother and his young heart- ' She kissed him slowly on the forehead. He felt the cool saliva that remained after she retracted. 'His tender eyes saw what happened. He's been living in daily torture and we are not helping him any bit.'

'Zwitt has a capable father and a not by any means less capable mother,' he defended. 'We are here to heal whatever wounds he incurred.'

He relived the young boy running over to the side of his dying Julie. He must have been terribly touched by the incident.

Lucy raised her head a little.

'Stephen, you have not as much as taken a look at your son,' she stated. 'This is not about us sweetheart. It's not even about wounds. It's about scars,' she emphasized.

'Zwitt is losing out to the memories of that tragic night. The house, the furniture- even us. We all haunt him. He has not even been eating.'

Stephen had noticed that Zwitt had shed a couple of kilos but that was as much as he could admit.

'I'll talk to him tomorrow.'

Lucy sniffed. This man wasn't getting it. She placed her head on his chest. She hated the thorns that he wore as hair on the chest but she endured tonight's repulsion.

'Zwitt needs more than a sermon. You shouldn't forget that he is your heir and he's going to be on the radar in the nearest future.' She swallowed some saliva. 'You can't allow people dissect him needlessly.'

Stephen listened.

'The little angel needs a change of environment, a set of fresh faces- faces he can relate to without bias. That is the only way we can rehabilitate him.'

'Lucy, I am not taking my boy anywhere.' He half-shouted. 'Whatever he needs, we get them here.'

Lucy traced the waist-end of Stephen's boxers and unfastened the rope. His hot-breaths returned in a flash.

'Whatever you want to do, never you forget that it's his vulnerable future we are battling to protect. Please take ego out of this,' she gently chided.

Stephen relaxed his will.

'So what are you suggesting?'

The rope had been unknotted. 'Let's find someplace where we can arrange for him to stay for a while at least- until his images clear.'

Stephen shook his head. 'We are not abandoning that little boy.'

Lucy kissed him- deep and thoughtfully. 'Of course we aren't. he would be under our supervision albeit indirectly.'

'There is enough love inside both of us to go round ten kids. For Julie's sake, Zwitt is going to get the most of our care.'

The shirt buttons were undone and her lips her eating at his nipple.

'Lucy,' he moaned. 'you know we owe Julie that much.'

Lucy was busy. She slid her left hand under his boxers, through the thick hairs and unto his brain box. Of course, they owed Julie. Was the whole family not built around her?

Everything was working wonderfully well. Stephen's hands were running freelance like a beast set free for the first time since puberty. Lucy bid her time again. She knew his limits and was going to be strict with him.

'Stephen. Stephen.' She had to call twice to catch his effervescent attention. When she did, she continued, 'Otima was here today.'

Stephen was shell-shocked. All the libido vanished in that instant. Lucy almost laughed out.

At that point, he remembered there was a bed-lamp and he put it on.

His delay may have cost him a lot, he admitted to himself. He sat up to talk with a pseudo-surprised Lucy.

9.12a.m. Sunday morning. Aswa Totle banged her knuckles frantically on the gate, simultaneously constricting her eyes to see through the slit-hole between both arms of the gate. More than every other thing, Aswa hated to be kept waiting- not to talk of kept stranded. She was a very detailed lady and after five months of futile knocking, anxiety was starting to build up.

Through the slit, she made out Bow's Mercedes 230E parked just outside the garage and despite all her twists and turns; that was the most her view allowed her. Bowono was either alone or perhaps he had company but even if he had the Princess of Wales with him, she deserved a heroine reception- not this.

Bow lived in the heart of the city- a far cry from what his status deserved. His home on Upper Strachan Street in Lagos Island was a middle-class newly renovated duplex. The crowded area usually had thin houses either stretched up or back or in both direction. There was a conscious effort to make maximal use of the available space. Buildings were so close together that lovers could even kiss across windows or to be modest, exchange soaps across adjacent bathrooms. It was not just the heart of Lagos, it was the bone. Groups of rough looking boys- the area boys loitered about speaking ethnic slangs and making gestures at friends and rival groups. There was nothing safe or reserved about the street. Her Boss-Bow would hear none of it. In his own opinion, those guys were better men than the police. They watched over everyone and with them, he could go to bed with both eyes shut; as long as he showed his generosity at regular doses. He was confident that they were faithful friends- nevertheless.

She evaluated her immediate surroundings. The Saturday night binge and parties had left mini-heaps of empty Alomo bitters bottles, juice cans and some used condoms. These people also partied hard- incensed by the routine free drinks and free for all indian hemps, the sound of their music usually blared till the early hours when the Imams started to recite their morning prayers. It was always one noise sidestepping for a newer- and often louder one. It amazed her how the 'responsible' ones managed to get decent hours of sleep. But then, it was their choice. So they had to live with the consequences.

In a predominantly Muslim neighbourhood, she was slightly surprised by the number of people who were scurrying to church. She felt a glitch of guilt.

What had happened to her faith? She had been trained up by her parents to honour Sundays. At home, they did Faith clinic on Tuesdays, dug deep on Thursdays, choir rehearsals on Saturday and crowned them all up with Sunday service. A routine she had ardently followed for the most part of her growing years but as soon as she gained independence, all signs of religion had disappeared. It was partly due to the pressures of her job. It was only in the phlegmatic rural areas that a young lady could have time for all those religious ceremonies. She had abruptly weaned herself of all the intra-week activities and held on to her Sunday-Sunday fellowship. Three months after she arrived Lagos and a month into her job, she had missed Sunday service twice consecutively. Rather than make atonements, she justified her truancy in her mind until it became a norm. These days, Sundays were strictly days for relaxing and catching up venom for the forthcoming days. Today she was still on her negligee on the sofa where she had slept off the previous night when Bow summoned her. That was about an hour ago.

People rarely got as they deserved. A fresh fatigue ceased her as she turned her back to the gate, leaning her weight on its frame. She was appalled at her very voluptuous esteem; she had literally paused her life to be here- jumped from one tricycle to another all in a bid not to keep her boss waiting for long. Why did the rich fetch fun in punishing the poor. What stopped Bowono from employing a gateman? She glanced around for a phone booth. There wasn't any yet. It was a Sunday morning and even non-Christians naturally slept a while longer. She had zero credit on her phone and sincerely, she had no energy to wander about in search of recharge cards. All the odds were against her. Aswa fastened her eyelids unsure of what to do next.

Just then, the pedestrian gate was unbolted and Bowono peeped out.

'Ah, Aswa,' he grinned. 'Who would have thought you had the energy to knock down gates?'

The humor was pale. She was silently glad she didn't embark on the fifteen minute walk back to the bus-stop without achieving her goal. She wore her handbag and walked past him into the compound. It was as she had seen through the gate- just Bow's car.

Aswa didn't worry. She figured that whoever it was could have come on foot or returned home with him last night. She walked in calculated steps but her adrenaline pumped.

Bowono read her mind with ease and just followed her. Women, he thought. Butterflies that thought themselves birds. Why would he call to invite her when he still had carcasses in his closet?

Aswa thronged into the sitting room. The door was partly open so she just had to shove it gently but she pushed it instead. She wasn't prepared at all for what she saw. Nothing. She turned, wide-eyed to Bowono.

'Why don't you tell me what your problem is?

Aswa knew her limits but something was driving her. She had no exclusive rights over Bowono Jereny but her curiosity cum jealousy fired her on.

She took off for the bedroom. As she ran, she could hear Bow repeatedly calling her back but she wasn't going to trade this thrill for some tepid explanations. There was just a singular mission; Find that mistress- that other mistress. It escaped her imagination that finding a mistress could result to a brawl- for which she wasn't equipped. Nor did it occur to her that she could earn an outright dismissal from her master's service. Nothing else mattered.

Once again, Aswa Totle flung the door wide open.

In Life, there were no good nonsenses. What had he gotten himself into? He had made one mistake too many and still, there was one waiting to be made.

'It's for the little boy.' Lucy's words had convinced him then but now, he wasn't totally sure if he was doing the right thing.

Stephen Avri wasn't certain that he could still tell Right from wrong. Otherwise how could he explain his deferment of disclosure of Julie's death to her family. Honest-ever his intentions were, it was certainly not going to help his cause. He had wanted to go to them accompanied by Bow but some way, he and Bow had been standing on highly-charged lines in the recent past weeks.

Presently, so many things had gone out of hand. His father-in-law had visited, obviously listened to a cosmetic version of the tragedy from Lucy and left without waiting to say a word to him. Lucy had played down on his reactions but he knew she lied. No father would take that news lightly- not the Otima he knew. Lucy sold him the impression that Otima understood perfectly when she made excuses for him. Stephen knew that some grave war was brewing. He wasn't prepared for confrontations. First of all, he needed to know who was on his side. He desired Lucy's support and the only frank way to win her over was to please her. He was in deep soup. He prayed the soup wasn't as hot as it was deep.

Stephen lazily climbed back into his car. He had chosen his Mazda jeep for today's exploit. The glittering all-leather interior blended with the alloyed wheels to an astonishing degree. He wanted his appearance to speak up even before him. He had worn a fitted sky-blue shirt- impeccably ironed alongside his well-tailored trousers. His seventy-three kilogram bulk and kettle-belly snug sweetly within the clothes. Just before he left the house, Lucy had offered him her 'Seduction'- the cherished perfume she usually wore. She wanted him to look like the donor he actually was. In fact the entire concept of dressing for the kill was her idea. She had instructed him of what carriage he should carry, the air of authority was vital for optimal co-operation. He was to talk and smile like a man who was in charge.

Stephen- the owner of the conglomerate needed no priming. Dominating his environment was not new to him but this was a different man. Lucy knew he was on an all-time low so she went the extra-mile. All she wanted were results.

Stephen opened the pigeon-hole and brought out the long list he had drafted from his Google search results. He gave it a pessimistic long stare and wondered how many more he would have to visit before he found a suitable home-replacement.

Seven homes and each looked a pole worse than the one before it. Something was wrong with the country's child-welfare system and he hadn't noticed up till now.

His first stop-over was at Special Ones- an acclaimed NGO dedicated to uncommon kids. Avri had been endeared by the name and had hoped it would be his first and only stop.

Half an hour of touring the facility convinced him beyond reasonable doubt that it really required Special kids to function within that enclosure.

The proprietor of the home had sincerely confessed to him that they were experiencing transient shortages in support and supply from international donors and sponsor firms. He had also quickly added that their prospects were brighter now than six months back.

The storey-building had twelve square rooms- eleven of which was home to seventy four years to fifteen year olds. The kids roamed about purposelessly like though autistic. The ones that came across him didn't even notice that there was a stranger in their midst. They seemed absolutely disinterested in any other thing but themselves or whatever activity they were engaged in. Stephen refused to adjudge them as rude. They apparently weren't taught any manners and nevertheless, they really owed no-one any apologies. The outside world had abandoned them. Why would they show 'uncommon courtesy'?

There was a diffused scarcity of everything. Inadequate staff, not enough food nor water. Stephen took mental notes of the bathroom. He could not stand any further inspections. The walls were smeared with greasy substances. He imagined that it could be faeces but there weren't many flies around the area. He concluded that the flies had probably eaten enough and had flown-aside for some power-nap. He turned around and this time, led the proprietor away. He tried to look into some of the kids eyes. Cold eyes.

Stephen was moved by the helplessness of their situation. He was unhappy that he wasn't assisting them in any way but there was one help he could swear he could render; he wasn't going to add to their figures. He wasn't going to add to the number of mouths that slogged it out for food at the Special Ones.

'I hope you'll be coming back,' the man asked. Stephen had forgotten his name the moment it left his lips. He had escorted him to the car and Stephen was certain it was the sight of the jeep that triggered his inquiry.

'Ooh. As soon as we are ready,'

The man wasn't convinced.

'Thanks so much for your time.' Then he added, 'Please take good care of them for me until-'

He knew the power of suspense and anticipation.

The man's brain would complete it '-until I come back.'

He had smiled and driven away.

At the outskirts of Shomolu, Stephen had seen another remarkable one- Sure Treasure Homes. After about an hour and half chat with the Manager cum Director of the facility, Stephen renamed it "Treasure through Kids Plc" in his mind.

It was a profit oriented home, funded by the owner and grossly independent of the wishes of the children nor their undertakers. Mrs Bankole was not the type to dance around the bush- she had engaged Stephen in a purposeful and very clarifying conversation.

'It's a bit like trading in the stock market,' she told him. Her name stuck in his head for two reasons; there was a bank in 'Bankole' and ole strictly translated meant thief. The female robber wasn't going to get away with her human trafficking for too long.

'Like everything in the market, children's values appreciate with time.'

'Are you confused over something?' she asked Stephen. He couldn't hide the awe on his face. 'Football academies train kids in soccer and invest in their careers,' she explained further. 'Schools are built to…'

Stephen was not listening. Here was a woman with all her milk of human kindness justifying her modern day slave trade by equating it to listed stocks in the market. It worried him even further that the Business premises didn't match the purported investment opportunity.

Sure Treasure was an apparently mismanaged stock.

The management certainly had a plan but the attitude of execution was suspect.

If he were to return, he was coming to round off the people-in-charge-someday.

A copy of Robert Greene's *48 Laws of Power* laid gently at the pillow-end of the neatly made bed. Aswa flung herself on the bed- even more exhausted than earlier on. Few seconds later, Bowono joined her in the room.

'What did you think you'ld find?' he teased. 'A half naked woman desperately clutching unto the duvet, her hairs standing on its ends and her eyes questioning the sudden intrusion?

Bow could be poetic at times. Aswa ignored the comical demonstrations and picked up the book. Laws of Power? Bowono? She had no inkling that he had the slightest regard for power. Her assumptions with Bow weren't quite reliable anymore.

She studied the hard cover. The power had been written in red. Laws were in green. She was the sort who saw meaning in colours and their combinations. Where red came after green immediately, it meant something different from where there was a word in white in between. Green after red was another scenario. Aswa wasn't suspicious but he had taken out five months to undergo a most mystical training on colour separation and interpretations.

For someone who utterly believed nothing about zodiac signs and their connotations to staunchly lend credibility to shades of colours, it was unusual. It was however a means of keeping her brain very pre-occupied. Whenever any set of dyes caught her intrigues, she would go the extra belaboured mile to interpret. Where she wasn't sure, she always consulted her textbooks once she got home.

Today, Red after Green with a white word separating them; she figured it expressly. A wave of envy had turned an innocent issue into a very bloody mess. She heaved. She was very accustomed to her interpretations making little contemporary sense.

'Aswa. You know I mustn't tell you but,' he paused to take her in. 'If you really want to know, I was in the toilet while you knocked. Hadn't pupuud in 3days so when this urge came, I wasn't going to pass it up for any bang.' He chuckled. 'And truly I haven't finished my business there. I had to take a break to let you in. Can't you see the door is still open?'

He unhooked his trousers as he walked towards the restroom. Aswa looked hard at the toilet, glazing her eyes round Bow to see the content- Nobody. She felt a quart of shame and some disappointment as well.

'It's ok,' Bow said, glancing back in good time to catch her head dropping. 'Please in the mean-time, feel free to use the fridge.' He entered the toilet and shut the door.

Aswa hissed. It had been days since she undertook the assignment for Bowono and the latter hadn't as much as called to ask her how she fared. It wasn't quite a herculean job but Aswa couldn't tie up his pre-task zeal and the lethargy that followed the execution.

Bowono had taken an entire evening to educate her on the essence of her mission. She had to blend the perfect carriage with the best words to milk out sympathy from Mr.Avri. It was only after she had assessed his heart that they could have a meaningful conversation.

'He has to feel connected to you somehow,' he had repeated. 'If you are going to score.'

Hours after the tutorials, Aswa had confirmed that Bowono indeed knew Stephen extensively. By her evaluation, they had quickly connected and even transmitted.

Her greatest worry was Bow's indifference; no check-up, no follow-through, just stark silence. It did seem like he had forgotten he assigned her a job. On several occasions, Aswa had been tempted to remind him but she resisted. As long as she had her results handy, she would persevere until he was ready.

Bow left the toilet and went into the sitting-room. He could tell that Aswa was lost in her own thoughts- whatever they were.

Bow returned to the room with a tray-full of bread and cheese, a pack of Hollandia yoghurt stood beside them. Aswa perceived the scent of the bread and she knew straight-up that it was home made. Bowono was tremendously resourceful and she envied him for that. It was apparent his undeterred exploits in domestic things gave him a sense of independence from women. He was not in a hurry to marry since he could obviously cater to his delicate needs.

She slid off her handbag from her shoulders and puckered her lips.

'Sunday morning martini,' she said. Some excitement was already creeping into her voice.

Bowono smiled and placed the tray on her thighs.

'It's called Breakfast in Bed my dear,'

This time, Aswa smiled back. She was already attacking the fresh oven-hot bread. Bowono gently took her bag and unzipped it.

'Were you successful?'

Aswa didn't understand at first. She turned around and when he saw him unzipping her bag, she understood.

'Successful with what?' she gurgled over a mouthful of bread.

Bow endured the wait. He had learnt not to rush good news especially with women.

'Did you see him?' He paused. 'Stephen, I mean.'

Aswa sipped some yoghurt and bit a smaller chunk of bread.

'Your Stephen is not as stern as you prepared my mind for,' she managed to say.

'That means you saw him.' Bow searched the bag more frantically. He wasn't feeling anything like what he wanted. He upturned the bag on the bed. All sorts of things came flying out. Mascara first then assorted eye pencils, three sizes of mirror, fairly-used handkerchiefs- apparently for editing facial make-ups. Bow shook the bag; there was something still heavy inside. He shook it harder and the pan-cake powder tray landed at the edge of the bed. It was his turn to be disappointed.

'Where is it?' He dropped the emptied bag on top of the mini-heap that had once been its content.

Aswa ignored his question and strolled for the refrigerator. The blend of yoghurt and bread was a little too thick for her throat. It was her time for power-play.

Bow watched her return with a half-full bottle of water. She had gulped to her fill at the fridge. She slid her left hand into the right cup of her bra and produced a micro-cassette.

'Is this what thou findeth?' she asked tossing it to Bow.

He gazed intently at the cassette as if he could read the conversation it contained.

'How was he?'

'Okay at first and then pale later.'

'How pale?' He was concerned.

'Paper pale or more precisely put, murderously pale.'

'So it was true?' Bowono asked absent-mindedly.

'What was true?' Aswa was confused. Bow's phone rang.

'Listen, I don't care what you say or do,' he shouted. 'Just don't call my number again.' He switched off his phone. He squeezed the button so hard that Aswa wondered whether he wanted to crush it. She stood wide-eyed at the door. The translation was brusque; one second she was answering a hushed interrogator. The next moment, an angry Bow was shouting into the phone.

He was a world-class dramatist.

'Am sorry about that,' he apologised. 'The idiot won't let me be.'

Aswa nodded and sat beside him. She also noted that he was quick to tender apologies and explanations today. Was she getting elevated in status or she had done him a grand favour- and she didn't even realize.

Bowono knew what drama he just played. The same reasons why he had deferred asking her how she went after so many days. He had had to shout to cover-up his stupid insinuations about Stepen's guilt. As much as possible, he wanted to eliminate bias.

'Did he say anything about me?' he asked. 'Any comment or question?'

'No, he just said he was expecting a friend,' Aswa replied.

Friend. So Stephen still called him friend, he mused.

Neho Dipo's Little Angels carved an image of an underused ship harbour. The serenity of its surrounding and the building itself drew an air of expectation as one approached.

Stephen Avri was slightly pleased to see something atypical. He couldn't estimate how long he had driven to get here but even the environment told him he was far from home.

He had hoped he wouldn't need to get to option no.11 before he found an appropriate setting.

The farther the better, he thought on behalf of Zwitt.

The high gates and fence and the cathedral-like building that perched at the south end of the compound was a sharp contrast to the any places he had dropped by today. Stephen wasn't sure they had built with a defined purpose. Perhaps they had fenced with the intention of building a prison, along the way- they had switched to erecting a church and eventually ended up with an orphanage.

As Stephen drove his car through the wide-open gates, he searched for any sign of life. There were strategically placed pointers that directed strangers on what direction to take. That erased the need for humans- to some extent. He imagined that there were stringent rules that kept housemates from loitering about.

The lawn immediately adjacent to the building was a delight. It had recently been mowed and the flowers were tailor-trimmed to write 'Little Angels'. Stephen was impressed. He was naturally tempted to think that they had done some urgent polishing to woo him but asides Lucy, nobody else knew he had undergone this search. Even she wouldn't have thought that he would go this far down in his list before getting a perfect place.

The main building was erected with bricks and although they hadn't been washed recently, it still learnt credence to the placid people he believed it sheltered. Still, there was not a soul in sight. He was starting to worry-really.

At the foot of the stairs, he killed his engine and stepped out. There were three cars parked around. One was a branded mini-bus and they all looked in use. He glanced around- now praying that he would see someone to inquire from. There was nobody so he climbed up to the only door he could see.

To Err is Woman

The door was huge- like the building and thick also- like most church doors. Stephen knocked hard the first time and found himself kissing his knuckles sorry. Before he could slap another round, the door opened and he stepped in.

'Good afternoon Sir,' an elderly man greeted him.

Stephen nodded. 'Please who is in charge here?'

The man motioned him to follow and without any further words, he spurned round as Stephen followed closely. The man was almost galloping across the long passageway. Stephen had to pace-up too as his curious eyes studied the house. He noted that there were doors on both ends of the alley. He had counted about fourteen, seven on each side when his guardian suddenly took a sharp turn on the left. Stephen almost stumbled. The shorter passage had just one door- directly opposite them. So far, the terrazzo floors were commendably clean although Stephen's meticulous eyes saw tiny pockets of assembled waste at various points along the walk.

Lightening was also adequate in the house. A few of the lamps were still on for very obvious reasons. So far, he had not seen a single window so he knew it would be absolute darkness whenever the lights went off. He was sure they often did but he could swear the facility owned a generator set. They seemed so efficiently designed.

At the door, the man stopped and knocked just once. Stephen stood impatiently behind the man for about five minutes. The man didn't repeat the knock and the door didn't open. He wanted to ask him to knock again but he dared not. There was something strange and overwhelming about their code of conduct. Was it discipline that set them apart or something deeper. He read the inscription on the door- over and over again;

NehoDiplo- Matron of Little Angels Home.

He didn't get this tactics at all. Were they trying to create value with delay or was there some sort of ritual that he was consciously getting entangled in. He was a busy man- an extremely busy man.

'Knock again now,' Stephen commanded. The man cursorily glanced at him and then firmly shook his head.

'Please, come right in,' a voice called from inside.

Stephen didn't hear the sound of bolts or keys turning. It was apparent that the door had been open all along.

Only Stephen stepped in to meet Neho Dipo.

The matron was a small-framed nubile post-menopausal woman. She wore a retracted face that appeared to be constantly musing over something. There were ferocious smears of make-ups splattered across her face that one would wonder if she didn't scare three year olds. Nevertheless, there was an underlying firmness to her person which compelled people to at least hear her out. It was this latter appeal that had seen her through the years. In spite of her negligible size, Neho was a perfect administrator, a master strategist in comparison with most of her contemporaries. She had trained herself to resolutely pursue any chosen cause to a logical conclusion and throughout her decade and a half affiliation to foster-home management, she had not one reason to regret. She prided herself as the mother of several now well-placed people- one of whom was Lucy Avri.

Little angel hadn't always been the gigantic structure Stephen drove into. Seven years back, it hadn't been Little Angels. One brilliant fact about her was her quick adaptability; she never shied away from wisdom- even when they came from foul mouths.

Without pre-information, nobody would guess that Neho had not even the faintest taste of formal education, no parental predilection to wealth and no congenital inspirations to set up such a monumental orphanage. More out of the absence of alternatives than passion, she had assisted Mrs Balogun twenty-six years ago in the latter's devout business of sheltering and raising homeless kids.

The whole scenario was a big joke. They had begun with eleven fat-appetite children who they literally had to go hungry to be able to sustain. Then the home was simply called "*Iya Balogun Home*" and in the years following its opening, the number of kids had risen as their means dwindled. Mrs Balogun was a genuine lover of children- the sight of suffering children of whatever race always triggered her sense of charity. It was sad that the trigger lacked a sensor. She got poorer and poorer as she sold off her personal possessions in desperate bids to keep the kids alive. It wasn't long before the sparse wealth that her late husband had bequeathed her disappeared.

In the fifth year of running the home, Iya Balogun passed away. The doctors said her death wasn't unrelated to Hypertension. Neho knew it wasn't unrelated to starvation and incessant worry from running the home. It was going to be the end of Neho's unsolicited romance with orphanages until Mrs Balogun's lawyer summoned her. The late woman had willed the head-aching orphanage to her. She was quite young then and unprepared for such huge responsibilities. Although most of the housemates were fond of her, she was not really involved emotionally in the art of keeping other people's children- especially when the gesture was grossly unappreciated.

The home was hers to keep or to spoil. She eventually made up her mind to try.

A lot of time had seeped across since then; concept changing time. In like rein, a lot of kids had slipped through her home; Special kids.

Now, she had one more visitor, the fifth for the day and the richest by a long pole. He could come in sheep's clothing or even as a sheep, it didn't matter to her. She already knew. He had come to suggest 'dumping' his son with them because his wife suggested so.

'Is this the matron's office?' Stephen asked, interrupting her thoughts.

'You couldn't be more correct,' Neho replied as she got up to shake his hands.

'That means you are- you are the Matron,' Stephen stuttered a bit stupidly.

'Or her imposter,' Neho finished. She accommodated his excesses.

'Neho Dipo,' she introduced herself.

'Stephen.' He intentionally kept his surname silent. He didn't want his host starting a "name-knot" tie game. If he had said his surname, the matter would have been different. In Lagos, there was just one Avri- as much as he recalled.

'Please do sit down,' she motioned him to a seat.

He sat down and perused the office. There were several pictures of kids all over the wall- mostly pretty children. Stephen noted a couple of ugly children and shrunk his brow naughtily.

Neho's desk was another concoction. There were well sort out files at the corners of the desk while directly before her were carelessly placed documents that she was apparently still working on. She did appear a very busy woman.

'I've got a baby for you,' Stephen went straight to the point. Neho stared at him, stunned. This Stephen was frankly nuts. She wasn't in the least enthralled by his choice of words.

'Isn't it obvious I haven't got any for you,' she said running her hands through her flat belly.

The incongruence was bare and threatening, Avri thought. She was equally naughty.

Neho watched him grin confusedly for a minute. They had to come to par.

'Sir, please what can I do for you?' she asked courteously. Her hands were pressed hard on the table as she leaned forward.

'First of all, let me commend the efficiency which I perceive you manage this home with. Actually, it's amazing seeing-'

Blablabla. Neho was not listening. She hated the whole praise-singing business and it was made worse by the fact that she had foreknowledge of what his mission to the facility was. All the same, she suppressed her displeasure and waited for the preambles to end. Finally, it did cease.

'What I want you to do for me is First-class, top secret- I mean classified but absolutely excellent catering albeit very temporal.'

Verbose man, Neho thought.

'I have a very lovely son-Zwitt.' He paused. 'I think he would need the attention of your facility anytime soon.'

Neho felt some contempt. It was not hard to see why Lucy despised this man. If he came to flaunt his flawless vocabulary, the sooner he discovered that he had the wrong audience, the better. Whatever words she couldn't pick were not said. That was her.

'Sir, it is possible we are overlooking something here,' Neho interrupted softly. 'Our facility is meant especially for the low-socio economical class kids, the destitute if I may use that word.'

'Especially,' Stephen re-echoed. 'Thank God you said especially. Having seen a fraction of what is on ground,' He chose his words more carefully. 'I feel it would be a wonderful experience for my boy in here.'

'If you say so,' Neho stated. She pulled her left drawer open and fetched a form. 'Please, kindly fill this form for me.'

Then she added, 'Sincerely'.

Stephen took out his pen from the breast pocket. The moment of truth had come- although a little earlier than he thought.

'So what have you got for your lad?'

Stephen was puzzled. Neho explained, 'If we take him in, what is the home going to get in return.'

'That boy means a lot to me,' he said blankly.

Neho waited for him to resume to no avail. 'So why don't you keep him with you?' She casually tugged at the form Stephen held.

'I think this home really stands to gain generously when they admit him.'

Late prophesy. She had already begun to reap off the vineyard even before Stephen drafted that list. If she played her cards well, there would be no limit to how blessed Zwitt's entry would make her. She knew about the Avri empire- everyone did and she knew the strength of Lucy- very few people did.

They just had to follow due procedure- for formality sake.

'Tragedy seems to have found us out.'

Bow recognized Stephen's voice. There had been few inaudible mutters before that statement. He placed the microcassette player closer to his ears and smiled gratefully at Aswa.

Aswa saw the smile and quickly reciprocated. She hoped her mission would be valuable to Bowono. In fact, she prayed so because for some queer reasons, she couldn't stand the thought of disappointing this man- Bowono Jereny. She watched him relax into the foam. He was as cute as ever, dark-skinned and with a tint that stood him apart from most men she knew.

He and Stephen had very identical accents and in retrospect, he admitted that the latter's own was more foreign. Bow's sparkling white singlet grabbed his averagely muscular physique and though knew how impossible it was-at least for now- she longed to rest her head on those broad shoulders.

Aswa more out of adoration than discipline discharged her duties to perfection. She prayed that someday she would drive her message home.

Bowono was her non-flinching boss, skilfully blind to the sparks he caused inside her. They hadn't worked together for too long before Aswa began to entertain wild imaginations. It was a matter of time and they would click.

So far, there had only been one chance but she had blown it. She hated the memory of that failed opportunity but at moments like this, it reared its head up.

Barely a month ago, she had been invited to their private office- this same room, to assist him redesign his crashed website. It was a job that demanded attention to little details as they stayed awake into the night, editing and restoring pictures where they belonged. They successfully acted oblivion to the passage of time.

Aswa after an unfruitful wait for Bowono to announce retirement plans for the day had been the first to voice out what time it was. 11.43p.m.

Bowono had glanced at his wrist watch and announced that they would be through soon.

Soon eventually became two hours later. By then, it was almost 2 a.m. Bowono had politely asked her to stay the night but she made the grand 'mistake' of rendering excuses that made what would have been her biggest night till date impossible. She had expected him to ask again but she never got a second chance to say yes. Indeed, her refusal had bruised Bow's ego. He had simply stood up and fetched his car-keys. What would have been the first of a series of breath-taking romances vanished.

My time will surely come…again. She relentlessly reassured herself.

So, what was she to Bowono Jereny? She hated it each time she asked herself that; the answers always gutted her.

She was the extremely dedicated and very efficient secret assistant. She was so proficient in her duties that it hurt her that Bow never mentioned the possibility of getting her a formal office. The terms of their contract- though orally read and consented to, strictly forbade any public show of acquaintance.

It baffled her why he didn't think of her in more superior roles- like a wife? She was the younger sister of Bow's ex. Did that automatically rule out their possibility of doing something serious?

They only enjoyed unsupervised company in his house and that was something she thought was slightly in her advantage.

She eased the arousing urge with a sip of water.

'She was what I call priceless but-' There was a clicking pause. Aswa remembered that moment. Stephen was utterly distraught and she could picture his face right now; the agony and hopelessness of an action that taunted his spirit.

'-she's gone. Killed by the same hands that swore to protect and love her forever.'

'Excellent work. Bravo, superb effort,' Bow was excited. He turned off the tape.

Aswa glowered. She was glad that he was pleased.

'That's why I usually can't express just how perfect you are,' he showered her more with praise. 'Multi-perfect, if there's any word like that.'

'Not nearly as perfect as you are, Boss.'

As typical, Bowono pretended not to notice the sensual flattery.

'How do I show you how thrilled you've made me?'

He got up to wear his shirts.

Aswa was disappointed. This man would habitually do the outright opposite of her desires.

Why wasn't he removing the singlet instead? She sighed subconsciously.

'However Sir,' she replied.

Always reserve business for business.

9

Stephen Avri's ink froze midway. He was detailing the excerpts of the most recent contract awarded to the Avri Construction Consortium by the State Government. There were no unusual figures, just the normal hundreds of millions. Monday was already deep spent and strangely, he hadn't seen nor heard from Bow. He adjusted his bow-ties and then decided to remove it. He needed some unhampered fresh air in his system.

It was against routine for Bow to bypass his office on reporting to work daily- not to mention when they had an a lingering score to settle. Bow always popped the door open to say hi before crossing over to his office.

Since the night of their foiled appointment, Stephen had intentionally ex-communicated him but even Bow had not made any visible attempt to assuage him. Very strange, Stephen thought.

He pranced across the office and then to the window. He could oversee Bow's car parked a couple of cars away from his. His designated parking space was empty yet he wouldn't park there- right by Stephen's. He walked back to his table, picked up the Intercom and then decided against it. He already had enough problems than he could carry alone. He needed his friend by his side at this critical moment.

He put on his tie again, straightened his clothes and his face and left his office. He had to climb two more storeys to get to Bow's office but he didn't mind at all.

Bow's door was partly open as he approached and his voice could be heard about two hundred meters away. He was on the telephone. Stephen had never had to knock to enter his office- although sometimes Bow did before entering his. The fact was that Stephen rarely had cause to come this way. It was usually Bow that showed more mobility.

'Hey,' Bow said drily dropping the receiver the moment Stephen entered. There was no panic in the spontaneous end to the call but Stephen felt the discussion wasn't concluded.

He just nodded to the Hey and took his place on the couch.

Bow had a lavishly furnished office, mahogany desks and office lamp stands that put a tinge of romance into the office. He placed two three-seater couches opposite his desk about twenty feet apart. The feel of the cushion was another way to say welcome to guests. The second mini-desk carried his newspapers. He was an ardent purchaser of dailies from different media firms and although he hardly had the time to read beyond the front pages, he never stopped refilling his newspaper table. In fact the papers had prompted his acquiring the seats because over time, the office served as some sort of readers hub for staff to convene during break hours. It was not surprising that Bow was more in touch with co-operate gossip as soon as they emanated than any other Avri Consortium staff.

The only advantage Stephen's office had to his was the view of the garage that his office enabled him. He wasn't going to trade that for any other.

Bow was dressed in an impeccable white shirt and a brown suit. It was an uncommon choice for his Monday. Stephen recognised the suit- he had practically forced Bow to buy that suit during their Singapore business tour about three years ago. Bow had little interest in corporate wears, he would rather put on his jeans and a T-shirt and enjoy the appeal it gave him. He said suits restricted him and Stephen had never asked him how.

Stephen slackened his ties again and started to unlace his shoes. They apparently had a long talk in the offing and he needed to feel at home. With a stretch, he stowed his shoes to the rear of the couch.

Bow watched him keenly. He seemed a bit clumsier than normal. Stephen hadn't come as near enough as to exchange handshakes with him. Asides the nod, there had been no communication between them. Bow was apprehensive that his stigmatised mind was driving rough. He tried to imagine what the usual Stephen would have done in the light of the prevalent circumstances.

He would have barged into his office and requested with a politely raised voice for explanations. They had of course had graver reasons to quarrel in the past but perhaps this time, his compromised mind had pushed him to act slightly differently. He didn't think in any case that it was his attitude that had changed Stephen's reaction.

Stephen was an indomitable icon- his mind was preserved in exclusive refrigerators.

Stephen's eyes followed his all this while and yet they never met. It was like they were fencing amidst rising tensions.

'What has gone wrong with you idiot?' he finally asked after over ten minutes of damning silence.

Bowono knew the question was for him but he couldn't afford to answer that.

They had called each other names at numerous occasions but this 'idiot' sounded a bit harsher.

'Bowie, you are getting on my nerves,' Stephen added. He got up and walked up to him. 'I must be frank with you. I have never been this disappointed in you. Never.' He finished.

Bow gazed into Stephen's eyes. The fury was resplendent in his eyes. He had rarely seen his temper break and even where they did, the issues were red grievous ones. Then his suspicious mind took over.

Had he looked this vexed just before he slew Julie? He wanted to scream back at his face. He wanted to state his own disappointment to his face.

'First,' Stephen continued. 'You fail to turn up for an appointment you scheduled yourself.'

Bow sneered.

'Inexplicably so and between then and now, the only apology you can render is by blowing cold- like nothing happened.'

Bow was unsure whether his conclusion was a question or a statement.

Stephen wasn't done yet. 'This- my dear friend- is not you.' He finished alas.

That was the beauty of his friend Stephen. He knew how to garner sympathy.

'Stephen, please can you sit down?' His voice was monotonously passive like he was speaking to someone who wasn't there. Stephen didn't move At all. He had sat back all these days and waited for Bow to call to explain.

'You came to get an apology?' he asked rhetorically. Bow stood up to face him. 'I equally demand an apology.'

He paused briefly. 'We agreed that we were to meet by 8.20p.m and you had the guts to accuse me to my face when I spent over three hours at Flavours waiting for you to turn up.'

'One. Two. Three.' He counted with his fingers for emphasis.

Stephen's brain was in jitters. 'Where?' he asked. 'Where did you say you waited?'

Bowono watched his confidence capitulate. A puzzled expression hung on his face. It was his litmus test. The old Avri was not the one who tricked with figures and words. Today, there was a huge crack.

Flavours or Forever's, Stephen couldn't vouch for any. It ricocheted in his head now. Flavours it seemed to say.

'I am sorry,' Stephen conceded. 'I suppose I was the dullard here. I made a headlong drive to Forever's,' he confessed.

Bowono let his jaw drop. 'Forever? That's a chip from the old brick. What could you have found there?'

'I am truly sorry,' Stephen repeated. Bow nodded him an okay. 'I never for once thought I could be the culprit on this case.'

Bow patted him on the shoulder. 'Please sit down.'

This time, Stephen obeyed.

'So for heaven's sake, what was Forever's like? Any old faces?'

Stephen shook his head. 'The usual-' He considered narrating what had truly transpired at the club but it was unnecessary. There were more pertinent issues at hand. 'Just displeasure.'

Bow nodded as he grinned. This man was remarkably as disintegrated as never before.

'So what were we going to discuss at Flavours?'

Bow stared at him hard and long. 'Time has overtaken those issues.'

Zwitt watched Lucy crumple a collection of filthy clothes into an old box. Her nostrils twitched in disgust at having to handle the damp smelling clothes. Nobody was going to do it for her. Besides, it always rang in her head that if she wanted a good work, she had to do it herself. There was no discrimination of dirty and clean one. The hitherto clean ones were not left on the air enough to dry.

Her wrist watch clicked on the box and the reverberation of the collision thrilled her. It was an old 'tinker' box- the same that once contained all her family ever had. The box had followed her down the years and she was delighted that at last, she could let it go. The splatters of red and black were still shiny although the edges had begun to know rust.

It was her parting gift for Zwitt and he was privileged to be the chosen one. There were chances Miss Dipo would recognise the box. Lucy had earlier taken the box to an artist to paint the eerie words 'Home Coming' under where she had boldly labelled Zwitt. She had her reasons for the showmanship and the box-bearer would soon discover why.

The cachectic kitten mewed its way into the room and then mounted the bed. It was a most audacious move by a cat that had been named after Zwitt- and just as maltreated. Of all animals, Lucy thought, cats were certainly the most forgiving. Otherwise, experience could have told Zwitty that she was too close to her predator. She didn't last a second on the bed. Lucy meanly grabbed her and flung her high and intently at the overhead fan. It was the nth time she was assaulting the little creature and her motive was clear. She believed the scenes always rubbed off on her name-sake.

This time she wasn't quite as precise as Zwitty missed the rotating blades. She however didn't miss the motor. She landed on her feet, utterly dazed.

Lucy was infuriated. The hope of seeing sliced out chunk of the kitten's body had enticed her. She launched to grab her again but the animal recovered in good enough time to flee.

Lucy chewed her teeth and scowled at her spectator-Zwitt.

His blank-stare and smile made her withdraw her gaze. It disturbed her that he had this elusive buffer. Zwitt recognized that look; trouble was lurking. He moved farther away and sat on a side stool, hoping he was reasonably out of harm's way. He was struggling to interpret what he felt.

All his clothes were being stacked in a box while he was dressed in the very best apparel he had- his last Christmas cloth. He really cherished the 'what else' T-shirt and the sky blue jeans over white canvas and he had not had the opportunity to wear it in a while. Once Lucy noticed his fondness for the cloth, she had seized it until today.

He was going somewhere but he had no clue where.

Lucy shot him a glance just in time to see the anxiety on his face.

'Get up snag,' she shrieked.

Zwitt shot up instantly, the brief fortitude he derived from Zwitty's narrow escape vanished.

Lucy drew him closer and whispered into his ears, 'You are going on a holiday- a lifelong holiday; No daddy and of course No mommy.'

Zwitt listened quietly.

'And the best favour,' Lucy continued. 'you can do to yourself is never ever coming back here.'

She bolted the box and pushed it to Zwitt.

'That's all you got.'

Zwitt hugged the box. If that was all he had, he had better guard it jealously.

He glanced up to Lucy. 'Is George coming too?'

'Strip that shit off your mind,' she screamed. 'You are all alone and I am sure that if you want company, you know where to get it.'

Zwitt innocently shook his head and then he remembered that such statements usually had bitter follow-ups. He started to nod vigorously.

Lucy rolled her eyes derisively. She wasn't going to let her chance to sting slip away.

After a brief hesitation, she started to whistle the now innate tune.

'Zwitt's Mama in Hell.'

With all of Neho's expertise in handling humans of all ages, there were very few encounters that got her palms sweating in nervousness. As she pressed the phone closer to her ears, streams of sweat trickled down her brows. It annoyed her to imagine that inspite of herself, her heart was beating at an alarming rate.

She couldn't let herself be intimidated by another woman's voice. There was little she could do but to pray for the call to end.

'You don't have to be afraid,' Lucy reassured her.

She might have heard her heart beat, Neho thought.

'Everything is carefully streamlined and all you'll have to do is to follow the orders.'

Neho nodded into the phone. She had a conviction that Lucy was seeing her.

What about the incentives, she shouted in her heart. Lucy had spoken for over five minutes and had made no mention of any monetary deposits. Those figures had been afore-concluded but she had stupidly not given Lucy a time frame. She was keeping her own side of the deal. Lucy had to step up. Yet, Neho couldn't voice her worries. She still had a huge chunk left from the refurbishing allowance that Lucy gave her over a week ago.

Experience had showed her that the Dragon Lady was best left to her will. She barely forgot anything; just that her timing was always supreme- ill or not.

Lucy muttered a couple of extra instructions and hung up.

The clouds turned dark all of a sudden and the strong wind threw dust and some mobile dirt all over the road. Stephen wound up his glasses and nodded Zwitt to do same.

They had left the house twenty minutes ago under an intense sunlight. The sickening tension between them had made the sun seem even more unbearable. The car's air conditioner had blown incompetently to the point that Stephen had resorted to natural hot air.

No one had foreseen the rain- not even the meteorologists.

Stephen flushed every worry in his mind. He was acting in the interest of the little mule and although he lacked the boldness to explain their destination to him, he hoped the young one would understand someday. From the rear view mirror, his eyes fell on the untidy box bouncing on the rear seat. He apologised within himself for not finding the time to buy Zwitt a befitting luggage box. Hopefully he would get him one as soon as his first visit. He had that strong temptation to say something to his son- no matter how vapid- to explain certain issues to him. Zwitt needed to know that he loved him extremely, just as much as he had loved- or still loves his mother- Julie.

There was a chance that Lucy had offered Zwitt a varnished version of the reason for his exodus. Avri sunk the temptation. He saved his voice for the moment they would exchange good-bye.

Zwitt sat all by himself and reckoned on Lucy's recessional speech. His heart bled to leave Geria, George and his progeny- Zwitty forever. He noticed wrinkles creep up and quickly vanish on his father's face and he struggled to catch his gaze to no avail.

The rain had begun to pour down and Stephen was carefully sinking into and jumping out of flooded potholes. Zwitt stared into the alleys by the road. All the pedestrians were scurrying for shelter. The very few that had umbrellas still found themselves non-immune to the hail storm.

Was the world all about refuge? Zwitt wondered.

'Daddy do I have a father?'

Stephen's concentration absconded for a second. He methodically shifted his gaze to Zwitt.

'Hmm,' he gasped. 'Of course you do.' More silence.

'How can you ask such a thing?' His tone was more emphatic.

Zwitt turned his small self to face Stephen. He was not intimidated at all. After all, he had seen more vicious monsters.

'Please, can you tell me where I can find him? I mean- my real father.'

Avri heaved as he tried to shelf his frustration. They were barely a kilometre from their destination. He steered the car away from the road and slammed the brakes.

For the first time since Julie died, he sincerely locked gaze with Zwitt and like he had always feared- the watery pleading eyes unnerved him.

He re-appraised himself.

'What's all this about?' he stammered. 'Did anyone say I am not your real father?' He was incredibly stuttering before his little son.

Zwitt obstinately shook his head, splashing emergent tears all over the car.

'I don't think you are,' he shrieked. 'Please just tell me where-'

'Zwitt, shut your mouth!' His father broke up his plea. 'Where did you learn such things from? Who has been talking to you?'

'Nobody,' Zwitt cried.

The tears rowed down his cheek forming some paste with the discharges already coming from his nostrils.

Stephen retrieved some tissue paper from his pigeon-hole. He held it against his nose and ordered him to blow.

'Zwitt,' he called. He was still sobbing so Stephen waited a while before he repeated the call.

'Yes Sir,' he replied.

'No, I want you to say Yes Father,' Stephen instructed gently.

Zwitt didn't respond. Stephen examined his first son closer. There were hints of chronic neglect on him. He hadn't bothered to look this hard at him since. He wondered what Julie would feel to see his Zwitt in this condition.

With a swipe, he lifted him to rest on his shoulders. It was a hug that healed both souls.

'Please, Zwitt dear. I want you to answer Yes Father,' he said pertinently.

Zwitt sniffed. 'Yes father,' he whispered.

Stephen drew him close to his chest. Even the rapid blinks couldn't stop the tears that loomed. He allowed them flow into Zwitt's scruffy hair.

'I think we should go home,' Stephen said withdrawing from the five minutes interlock. 'We've got some catching up to do.'

Catching up. The words loomed in Zwitt's head. That wasn't possible; not with a Lucy standing around!

Stephen reversed the car and piously returned to No.9 Julius Nyerere Street Adejo Lagos.

The clouds were much brighter now.

10

An ominous silence hung over No.9 Julius Nyerere street. There were strangers in the house too. Geria and George stood out in the corridor as directed by their mother. They had only heard as much as the odd men inquiring after their father. And they smelled trouble. None of the strangers had a pleasant voice but their mum appeared so at peace with their presence.

As they awaited Stephen's return, the policemen sniffed around the house and in-between moments, they interrogated Lucy in whispers. She was remarkably happy that they had come- and at the idealest time too. Stephen having given out Zwitt would come back to meet his own arrest. There was little fuss about it- there was God's divine hand in it all, ordering all the affairs of women. All she needed do was to sit back and enjoy the drama.

The mufti dressed law enforcers had walked into the compound as soon as Stephen drove-out. They were lucky that Lucy had delayed pressing the lock button on the remote so the gates had been wide open as they entered. They had in fact been awed when the gates started shutting on its own right after they had driven in. It appeared like they had walked right into a snare but they kept going, turning with the trees and staring around in search of a residence. Eventually, there was one in view. It was only at that point that A.Y Rizi anxiety waned. There was no single thought that hadn't crossed his mind the moment the gate shut on its own. He wondered whether the Police Force had eventually marked him out for elimination. No one would blame him for expecting the worst. He had received an early morning summon from the D.P.O and then instructed to escort an officer he had never met before to the Avri residence. The superior officer- now his partner had been sent from the State Criminal Investigative Department. They had proceeded on the 'mission' in anxious muteness even up till this point. Rizi just followed him; he so loved not being in charge.

Lucy didn't need to be told who they were. She had garnered enough experience to recognise policemen at first sight. The hurriedly shaven jaws and lean faces punctured with very fake smiles and insatiable deep-seated hunger usually gave their identity away. They always had their noses in the air, prying for food and then crime or the crime that will bring food. In between both craves was their sheathed love for women. They can love women!

'Your quest is timely,' Lucy whispered, making sure he caught the junior officer's gaze. He quickly removed it. She was a mistress at eliciting petty jealousy from paranoids. She knew the officer that introduced himself as Tunji was the senior one and hence would demand more attention. She knew she would create some latent clash when she pretended to show more interest in the scrawny looking Azri.

'Timely,' Azri repeated.

Stupid officer, Lucy made a mental note. That was all he had done since they came in; repeat the last words anyone said.

'This was where he hid for over twenty minutes o,' Lucy pointed at a corner of the passage. She then walked over to demonstrate. 'We kept on imploring him- Stephen come out nah, but he wouldn't until he was ready.'

'How come you haven't come to make a report at the station?' Philip Tunji asked.

'Which station?' she asked rhetorically. 'I called in on the night it happened.'

A.Y froze. Karma had revisited him. He knew he had to re-direct the story if his neck wouldn't be on the line.

'Madam, how have you managed to stay here- knowing full well how endangered your life is?' This was his first original statement and they came out in monosyllables.

Lucy heaved. The stupid officer wasn't too stupid after all. She took them on her recitation marathon. How Stephen had crippled her with threats, how she had been ostracized from her family, how Stephen had decided irrevocably to give out his son for adoption and how she feared for her own kids. She as usual didn't seem the least desperate for help but there was a vague identity that marked her out as the victimized wife of an affluent husband.

By the time she was done, A.Y Rizi was sniffing to withhold tears.

'Please let me get you people something to eat,' she added almost immediately.

They dared not refuse and she excused herself to the kitchen.

'Pretty woman,' Tunji said. Those were the first words he was saying directly to Rizi.

The latter nodded. 'Woman,' he murmured.

Tunji shook his head. He didn't quite understand what was wrong with his partner but he hoped their partnership was not going to get consummated at the C.I.D.

Tunji brought out his jotter from his breast pocket and then sketched what seemed like the living room on it. Rizi sniffed in his heart. Showmanship.

Lucy summoned them to the dining table.

'Your husband is indeed very famous in this area,' Tunji mumbled. A shovel of spaghetti was in his mouth already.

'I hear that a lot. He was indeed a successful man,' Lucy said. She sat directly opposite the men and sustained eye contact with any at will.

Both officers heard the 'was' but it struck no reason to object. There was a sauce of dodo gizzard and very fresh fish beside it. That was the language that counted right now.

Tunji had known Mr.Avri for a little above four years. It was a seamless four years- just courteous calls that usually left his pockets well-greased with innocent tokens of goodwill. He hoped that Stephen wouldn't recognise him in this circumstance or his work might be compromised.

Recognized or not, there was sincerely very little it would change. He was currently following orders and sympathy was way out of the question.

'When we got a report from his in-law,' Tunji continued. He was fond of talking most when there was food in his mouth. 'At first we thought the old man had gone insane. It didn't seem possible that a crime of such magnitude would be pushed under the carpet for so long.'

A.Y Rizi shivered again. That was just why Nigeria just had policemen while America had cops. Why would this Tunji refuse to leave this matter of report or no report?

'I think she has been living in fear,' Rizi stepped in again.

Tunji nodded. 'It must have been hell.'

Lucy saw her chance again and she took it. She explained how she had sneaked out to the village to inform the deceased parents.

'It was heart-breaking seeing her parents take the news of the tragedy. I mean who wouldn't be aggrieved, having such a lovely daughter and then hearing that she's been hacked down all of a sudden by her husband.'

Rizi heard the 'hack' and he subconsciously felt for his gun. His mind was on a fast track. Whatever monster this Stephen was, why would he deal so cruelly with women? There was a trace of goodluck lined in their mission.

He did the arithmetic. If they arrested Stephen, he had a chance to become Lucy's confidante. She was putting up a bold front but he knew she would need protection. There was no imaginable protection better than a police husband's. He had a fair chance but Stephen had to go first.

A.Y Rizi shifted nervously on his seat. Lucy's gaze was lingering more on Tunji. That was always the problem. Whatever he fancied usually fancied another but him.

This wasn't quite about fancy. He was planning his future at this moment and no bloody policepapa was going to foil his plans. He glanced across the house and swallowed hard; the prospects of eventually getting married to the perfect woman were overwhelming.

'Zwitt, Zwitt,' Geria shouted as she galloped down the stairs. She had forgotten that her mother had ordered her to remain on the terrace upstairs.

Lucy made a 'you see how much we love him' face at the officers. She had herself pressed the enter button for the gate some minutes ago when the sensor noted that Stephen was approaching.

'We begged him not to take that boy away but as usual, he wouldn't hear any of it.'

The policemen shook their heads. It was action time.

Geria unbolted the door hurriedly and ran out. She was still chanting his name. The effects of the passion was vital for the strangers' impression. Lucy waited for the little one to run back utterly disappointed. It didn't happen so she peeped through the window and indeed, there was Zwitt's tiny head in Stephen's car.

Gosh, Stephen was joking with her.

In any case, she hissed and stumped upstairs. There were bigger cards to play.

Zwitt was pleased by Geria's unprecedented reception. She acted like someone had told her she would never see him again. Stephen watched the two lock in a passionate embrace and he was convinced he had taking the right decision. Geria didn't even acknowledge him- but even that was okay. He winked and walked into the house. He hadn't seen the officers' car because Lucy had earlier asked them to re-pack in a rather hidden corner in the compound.

'Excuse me Mr Avri,' a voice said from behind him as soon as he stepped in.

He spun around. The voice was flat and unfamiliar.

He quickly studied the men and then glanced around for Lucy. She was not in sight.

'Yes, I am and how can I help you?'

He walked to the nearest sofa and sat down. The men followed him closely behind.

He knew they were police officers; he knew them even if they came naked. His heart thumped.

'Please Sir. You are to follow us to the station immediately,' A.Y enthused. He was indeed in a hurry to get rid of his main obstacle.

'What station? Are you arresting me?'

The men didn't reply him. Tunji was angry that the junior officer had read the 'arrest warrant' without his permission.

'For what reasons?' Stephen further probed. He carefully avoided using the word 'offence'.

'You will find out once we get there.' Rizi finished firmly.

Stephen arose gently. His tough times had just begun.

Sulli O'hib sank with a thud into the chair and double-screened the restaurant. The lightening was seductively dimmed and it was apparent that he hadn't been noticed unduly. He was bound by his profession to stay alert.

This was his second election year and by virtue of his rising profile, the stakes were much higher this year than four years ago. He knew he was a wanted man but his time wasn't up yet. He brushed the uneasiness aside and studied the tables around. His nearest neighbours were four tables away and they were engrossed in a seemingly legal conversation as suggested by excerpts that his ears clung unto. Their voices rose and fell as they traded words that were of no obvious threat to Sulli.

He searched the inside of his jacket and retrieved a stick of his brand; Rothman's- the best a paranoid mind can buy. He re-evaluated himself. He was a well-priced eraser and highly sought after especially by his 'old customers' and those who wanted to terminate his career. Most of his new contractors came by recommendation and that had at first worried him. It bothered him that the new ones would someday be snares that would ultimately engulf him. As a precaution, he had it as a rule that the recommender must call to confirm that he had indeed given his contacts out. In any case, business was good.

Six years into the field, he wasn't done yet. There were plenty of luxurious years ahead- if truly a labourer deserved his wages. At the moment he was content with just working, improving in zeal and competency with every new job.

He retrieved a neatly folded paper from his left pocket and re-studied the room before laying it on the table. It was his mobile Curriculum Vitae and he took a great measure of pride and confidence in perusing the twenty names on the list. The more recent inclusions were political stalwarts and he made some notes about their identity beside their pictures. Carrying this stuff was quite risky. He knew they were instant implicates but they were necessary for effects especially when he was meeting a new hand. Sulli was convinced he hadn't done his greatest job yet.

That one job that would bring him fame and money and very likely- an instant retirement. He craved for that legendary status. He was good in the art and all he had to do was to wait for the time to blow. He was optimistic that after his era, the mere mention of his name to stubborn kids will get mothers an instant reward. That was his idea of Legendary!

He put the CV back into his pockets and tilted his head backward, his neck anchored over the back rest. His half-closed eyes were traditionally more sensitive than any other person's open eyes. He wondered why ladies were always late for appointments.

Sulli O'hib was a bulky black complexioned assassin. Back in the years, he was a fiercely loyal Mama's boy who had nursed the ambition to become a doctor. Growing up, his mother had over fed him with stories of how academically distinct the father he never knew was. His father was a Physicist – the half-literate mother pronounced it as 'Fusicist'-whose addiction to undertaking risky ventures was unrivalled. The mother never ceased telling him tales on how the more western scholar had opted to lend his brilliance to the Biafran fellows during the civil war and how he had pioneered the invention of the first locally produced weapon of mass destruction. It was clear that he had been her hero and very certainly had tickled her fancy with exaggerated exploits of his participation in the war. After the war, the man had stuck to staying in the Middle Belt where he pursued a career in Demonstrative Physics. Of course, the latter words were beyond Sulli's mother. He read up those from archived files that belonged to his father. However Wee Ohib's 'Fusicist' had met an abrupt end while demonstrating explosive handling techniques to a host of final year Physics students. It wasn't the most daring of his exploits but tragedy was just destined to befall the young family. He had died from high-grade burns, alongside all the students leaving behind a toddler son and an ill-prepared wife.

Sulli knew that sad story down to his breaths. He had promised his mum that he was going to wear his father's shoes. In a broader sense, he sometimes felt he was making good his promise. His father manufactured explosives, he utilized them.

Seven years ago and prior, he was an astute disciple of honesty, contesting the virtue in every act of his; Even in wearing the right hair size on his head.

He was divinely raised and resolutely protected by an extremely doting mother from a child-hostile neighbourhood. His brilliance in school marked him out as the son of his father and he made seamless progress towards becoming the child of promise- a medical doctor.

To Err is Woman

Sulli spent all his early years shielding his mother emotionally from any manner of hurt. He did that for as long as she lived.

Peer-pressure was a huge issue in their militants-infested Warri area of Delta State. Neighbourhood gangs and counter-gangs were always on one another's throats yet Sulli managed to heed his mother's advices. He was barely heard but not an invisible loner. The gang niche knew he existed but they couldn't fathom why he isolated himself from extra-academic issues. At some point, it was rumoured that he was mentally setback- a worry he had shed with his mother. Wee O'hib in her characteristic manner had waved the rumor away and reminded him that he was better than all the boys put together. That reassured him a great deal.

Sulli only spent less than a tithe of his time in his mother's provision store. It was more kiosk than shop but Wee wanted minimal contact between the upcoming hoodlums and her son. Still, it was in one of his rare visits that trouble brewed.

That evening, Tough Gun –an arch member of the Gunners had come to the shop obviously in search of a brawl. Sulli was manning the shop alone at the time and in spite of the flurry of hateful words from his customer, he had kept his calm.

'Kolo, get me a pack of Ganja,' Tough Gun had ordered.

Sulli stretched forth a pack of cigarette to him. Tough gun smashed the pack to the ground.

'Omomo, you no know wetin be Ganja?' he bellowed.

The other Gunners- Slim Gun, Dry Gun, Sharp Gun- all burst into laughter.

Sulli stared at the scattered sticks of cigarette on the floor and bent to assemble them.

'Idiot, no be you I dey communicate?' Tough Gun presses as he crushed the sticks closest to his shoes.

'I am sorry. This are the only ones we have.' Sulli explained pointing at the floored merchandise.

'You wan teach us English?' Dry Gun stepped in. 'You wan prove say your stupid mama teach you–'

Dry Gun never finished the question as Sulli back-hand slapped him mute. He was obviously not prepared for that.

In a flash, all four Gunners were on Sulli. Their voices blared across the shop but none dared to touch him. They had never seen him this agitated and even the sight of it delighted them. It was pleasant knowing that this Mama's boy was just as gullible as they were. The imprints from his slap was still on Dry Gun's cheeks. As their tempers flared, Sulli waited for them at the crest of the ladder. He was not at all scared of the impending duel.

'Sulli Ohib.' Wee's loud voice rang through the tension.

All five youths sprang their attention to the piercing summon. Sulli recognised the mother's voice and interpreted it accordingly.

He remembered that she often told him that real men ought not fight to prove their status.

Sulli swallowed hard and long until his fury dissipated. He bit his lower lips and side-stepped the intruders.

'Today is your lucky day,' he said to no-one in particular.

The Gunners nodded in cruel understanding. Sulli O'hib would fight them, beat them and perhaps kill them– if his mother wasn't there. That was their deepest desire. They so longed for that vicious battle with the 'innocent Sulli'.

After the near-clash with the Gunners, he had brushed aside the incidence. He anticipated a second brawl but it never occurred to him that the Gunners would force such brutality down his throat. On the fateful night, he had persuaded the Mum to allow him attend a Christmas Carol. She had reluctantly agreed and for the first time in her life, she had gone to bed without having to check whether her son was already asleep and to kiss her goodnight.

She never managed to wake from that sleep. Her screams had pierced the stillness of the night as the Gunners had sneaked into her bedroom and sent her home with fatal slashes and stabs of their knives.

A glance at her corpse on his return and he knew who the assailants were. He couldn't tuck away the guilt of being absent at such vintage moments. For a mother who was always there for him, he had no valid excuse. They had slaughtered her like a snake- slowly and painfully until she died. He could never erase the image.

When Tough Gun's badly mutilated corpse was found suspended from a local bridge about twenty fours later, the rest of the Gang knew they were in for a Black Christmas. The corpse was designed with hateful cuts and crushes. It was hard to say what the weapon of execution was but like Wee's corpse, there was no bullet wound.

They took to their heels.

At the completion of three months, Sulli had tracked down the last of the animals- obtaining repetitive confessions and pleas for forgiveness in each execution. With each recount, he was reassured that Wee would be pleased that he had taken up the responsibility to avenge her death.

Sharp Gun's headless body was unceremoniously displayed in front of the Kaduna State Government House. He was the one who had run the farthest and yet Sulli found him and paid him in his own coin. Only Sulli knew what he did with the head.

His first series of murders was all the baptism he needed. His mother was finally gone and her vengeance completed. Strange enough, he yawned for more exploits. There was something exciting about being in utter control of another man's life.

Six months after Wee passed away, Sulli turned professional. The media had branded the job an "Expert's Deed". He was confident he could only get better in the art until he retired as a legend.

A pair of curious eyes had been studying him. He could feel the warmth of their penetrative gaze. Sulli slowly opened his eyes and returned the stare. The lady was not deterred. Sulli recounted the number of tables that separated him from the exit door. He had deliberately sat a table short of the twelfth they had agreed on. That was probably why the lady seemed a bit confused.

Sulli sluggishly stood up and moved to the appropriate table, monitoring his assumed client with his hind eyes. The relief was imminent on her as she hopped to her feet and swayed magnificiently after him. Sulli sat down with a heave and watched her glide towards him. He enjoyed working for ladies with non-retractile beauty. He loved it.

Sulli settled lightly on her chair and nodded absent-mindedly to Sulli's hello. She had been delayed in the excess of an hour by the dumb assassin. She silently lent her support to the Federal Government's insistence on Universal Basic Education. Every damn idiot needed some preliminary education. She maintained her stern face burrowed with her innate uncompromising character. There was no need for pleasantries so she excluded them entirely.

'You kept me waiting,' Sulli threw the first stone.

'What kind of nonsense talk is that?' Lucy began her onslaught. 'I just can't understand how you managed to make out a profession by killing people far better than you will ever become.'

Sulli smiled broadly as he excused her. She still looked radiant even in her fury.

Lucy noticed the strange smile and stopped the rant. No matter how bad this man was, he knew that his customers were always right.

After a brief pause.

'Are you as good as the rumours suggest?'

'Rumours,' Sulli replied smacking his lips 'are believed only by fools.'

On another occasion, Sulli would have just won himself a resounding slap. Tonight she let her eyes batter an unscathed Sulli. He loved to sting pretty women with words.

'I understand you still maintain a hundred per cent record.'

'You understand?' Sulli asked. 'Who was your instructor?'

Sulli knew there was no mystery to how he got his clients. He wanted to test her ability to keep secrets.

'The contact has been made. We are the two factors here- no extras.' He added the last with an emphasis.

Lucy watched Sulli roll his eyes and then yawn.

'I suppose you are right,' he conceded as he searched his pockets.

Lucy silently prayed the beast didn't want to smoke into her face.

'That's my CV,' Sulli said dropping something on the table.

He even knew CV, Lucy thought with keen contempt. She stretched her hands and collected the paper on the table.

Sulli watched her with keen interest. She unfolded the paper and her eyes instantly lit up.

Lucy recognised the first face and swallowed very hard. the name was scribbled underneath the photograph. It was he.

Alhaji Dawaka Ibru, General Manager of the Dawaka Enterprises- a foremost Cocoa-processing company headquartered in Benue. Lucy knew the rest by heart. He was hacked down on August 23rd 1997 en-route his daughter's wedding ceremony. Lucy memorized the date because she had been a guest at the occasion. Even up till yester night, the police were still looking for people who would volunteer any form of clue as regards resolving the murder and hunting down the killers. Lucy frowned. Killers indeed?

Sulli saw the spontaneous trickles of sweat on his client's brows. She had been caught off balance by his exploits.

'You are splashing so much time on one.'

Lucy shifted her gaze to the next..and quickly to the third. The palpitations were clawing into her throat. She had to stop. There was something peculiar about his targets. They were high-profiled killings and glorified unsolved murders.

'That's all for intimidation?' she scowled returning the 'gallery' to him.

Sulli O'hib nodded. He could perceive that she was shaking inside.

'You did all that-and got away with it?' she stuttered.

'That's why I am here,' Sulli took over. 'I believe you need me to help you get rid of something. Why don't we get down to the ditties?'

Lucy zipped up her anxiety- as much as she could.

'Actually, before I saw that CV, I only wanted something bloodless-'

'Bloodless?' It was Sulli's turn to get jumbled.

'Yea, Something like an abduction.'

She saw Sulli's frown deepen. 'But since you are this efficient,' she continued. 'We can handle it your own way.'

The assassin chuckled. 'That's the way it is then. Four hundred thousand now, five hundred after.'

'Cedis or Naira?'

Sulli mean stare answered her ridiculous question.

'That's a whole lot,' Lucy gasped. 'He's just a boy and you have no security system to worry over.'

'I understand,' Sulli nodded. 'Every life is as valuable as the other and frankly if you want someone dead- the person must be worth the risk.'

Lucy listened. 'The most important thing is that the bug is removed forever,' he finished.

Lucy cursed him under her breath. She didn't need any lectures.

There was no justification to having to spend that fortune just to eliminate a mosquito. Not when she could procure rat poisons and other crude means. Her temper was soaring.

'I'll get back to you,' she hastily said as she scampered away.

11

Tender Love and Care Schools celebrated its two years of existence two years ago. Its profile had rapidly soared as an entrenchment of celestial academic achievements. With a staff strength of eighteen teachers, four gardeners, a gate keeper and three clerks, all neatly fitted into two widely spaced two-storey buildings.

The classes were arranged to represent the corresponding strata and the recent construction work at the other end of the compound strongly suggested that a college would be added to their feather soon.

In the last three years, the management had steered the school to the social class they desired. The children of the average man were scarce to find. The fees were not structured to favour such nor were the rules. Pupils at TLC were never flogged except on parental request or pre-approval. Teachers were often silently subjected to spells of punishment and an invisible air of fright always hung about the school premises.

Zwitt was in the third grade. He had loathed the eventuality of entering the third grade- perhaps because it represented a transition from the traditional pencils he had used from nursery school to Second grade. It had meant that he wouldn't be able to clean his mistakes as often as he liked.

Not unusually, his marks nose-dived in the first term. His confidence was ebbed and he struggled to find his feet until he was accosted by Tolu. She was the bright pupil of the class and in spite of their ages, she quickly noticed that all wasn't well with Zwitt. TLC had a habit of mixing pupils up randomly per session but the bright brains still knew themselves. Tolu knew Zwitt had been smart up to the Second grade.

At that time, Zwitt was being himself- exposing his eight year old sensualities to anything that tickled it. It had been rumoured that one of their classmates always wore torn pants to school. It was essentially a boys' rumour but the consequence was that boys had a daily routine of throwing their pens down right in front of the little girl and bending over to pick them. It was a 'healthy' leisure for most of the boys who had no hither knowledge of such pleasures.

It was in one of such ventures that Tolu arrested Zwitt. She had whispered some kind words into his ears- though he couldn't recall what exactly- and they had formed a formidable tag team since then.

Zwitt's performance gradually rose; at least he took second in that term's results.

Now this was third term. Surprisingly, there was no Tolu. She hadn't come back to the school after the vacations and there was no-one to ask. Zwitt had also lost his mother during the holidays. He was stranded on all fronts.

Zwitt Avri sat back conspicuously on his seat and watched his classmates scribble down hurriedly formed words on their notebooks. Though he avoided her eyes, he felt Miss Sowofa's bemused stare at him from time to time. His near-blank sheet was placed listlessly on his desk and although he had boldly written the topic- MY TRUE HERO- on the top corner, it was apparent he was unwilling to go further than that.

Miss Sowofa had given them a pre-emption about two days ago that they would be writing on this topic and as such the kids had gone to town with the expo. At the moment, the demanded ten sentences seemed like minced meat for most of them.

That was the least of Zwitt's problem. He was undecided on the best string of sentences that would translate his emotions.

To Err is Woman

He allowed his eyes the luxury of dwelling on his neighbour's composition.

Terre was already on his seventh point. There was something about his diction, Zwitt noted. Zwitt decided to read after switching the pidgin translator part of his brain on.

My True Hero na Clement.

Zwitt rolled his eyes away in a futile bid to avoid reading more. It was not unusual for Terre to sidestep laid down rules.

Second line. *Clement na my man for life.*

His lucid handwriting helped demystify his choice of 'pidgin' English- a brand of English highly forbidden in the Avri household.

What had happened to Terre was simple. While most pupils had returned home to his parents with the now viral question, Terre's parents had not as much as found time to see their son- not to mention entertain his assignments. He had instead found an Audience with their houseboy- a sharp self-trained Calabar boy. The rest was history being enacted today.

Zwitt was bemused with the write-up.

Line 10.

Clement na pesin wey no de dull at all at all.

His ink froze as he shifted his sheet off Zwitt's field of vision. Then he stared back squarely at him. The friction was resonant.

Miss Sowofa noiselessly walked over to Zwitt's table. She nursed the fear that the little boy if unaided may necver overcome the tragic loss of his mother. It was on her insistence that Lucy failed in her bid to demote Zwitt to a lower class for 'compatibility' reasons. She had expressed her firm belief in front of the school administrators that Zwitt would bounce back to his usual bright self. Her bargain was certainly not going to pay off like this.

He was still her favourite pupil except that each time he was tortured by the abstract, she feared for her stand. The torture was becoming more frequent of late too.

She pulled Zwitt's blank answer sheet from under his left forearm, jolting him simultaneously. As she glared over the page, her displeasure was exaggeratedly expressed.

'Zwitt,' she called. 'This is all you've got for your true hero?'

Zwitt deflected her strong scrutiny as he shook his head. Angry tears lurked at the edge of his eyes as he anticipated more embarrassments from a teacher who had been so nice to him.

Miss Sowofa didn't wish to drive things that far.

'If you've got something,' she pleaded. 'Anything at all, please put it down.'

Zwitt nodded.

'You have barely two minutes.'

Zwitt picked up his pen and began to sequester some genuine blend of words.

Perhaps they wouldn't be as great as his teacher wanted them but they were sincere and more importantly, by the rules.

She is no more.
Not that she could not stay.
But she had to go.
Early, so early in the day.
I can still hear her telling me.

Zwitt counted the lines and continued.

That when I've got any problem.
I shouldn't just sigh.
Forgetting to take them to God.
Time may have gone.
Still, my mother remains my True Hero.

He savoured his work; there were certainly going to be errors but he was relieved he had poured out his heart. He arose to submit his sheet to Miss Sowofa.

Zwitt's essay kept her breathless for a while. Before she could take her eyes off the paper, he was already back on his seat- his dark watery eyes firmly rested on her.

The boy was indeed his mother.

Bowono swam smoothly to the pool stairs and grabbed Lucy's water soaked thighs. She shrieked and Bow playfully tugged her back into the pool. They swam abreast to the opposite end. It was fairylike- she was lost in his grip until the quarrelsome voices permeated their sanctuary- stripping off the temporal bliss.

'Why did you bring them along,' he whispered into his ears. There was a measure of disgust.

'They've got to learn how to function around you,' Lucy explained humourlessly.

'Not while we are still groping to know each other?'

Children, Bow thought to himself. He wasn't sure he could stand them.

'But they are not interfering.'

'Of course they are not,' he replied sarcastically.

George's light footsteps and tearful pants got closer. They exchanged a knowing gaze. Lucy knew the children disrupted their privacy but Bow had no rights to talk of her kids like they were household pests.

He disentangled himself from her and paddled tot the edge of the lavishly decorated pool. It was supposed to be a Sunday afternoon make-out for the both of them. He had chosen Lekki View hotel because it offered them the serenity they required and indeed, he owed this pool a lot. Most of his intuitions had come while he lurked inside the water. When Lucy had arrived with her baggage, he had quickly hidden his disappointments. He had instead asked the hotel guards for the children's playground and then requested that the kids be ushered there. That was why it irritated him seeing them returning less than half an hour later. There were so many things he couldn't do with their mother in their presence.

The wisdom of life consists in the elimination of paltry emotions, he chided himself.

'George Washington, come and tell me the problem,' Bow lured George.

The boy stood still for a moment searching for a nudge from the mother's eyes. She too was surprised by Bow's sudden reversal of attitude. Alas, George walked towards him.

Lucy smiled as she watched both men tackle their issues. She could see Geria sitting indolently under a shade. That girl was one of her secret worries. She was never keen of family and Lucy couldn't recall the last time she saw her merry- the way most innocent children were. She cast the picture of some violated child. Lucy shelved the worry and returned her attention to the other end of the pool.

Bow had successfully soothed George and his eyes were on his little legs as he walked away. She could trace some love in his stare. If Bow could accept her children as his, her problems would be a quart-solved.

'Bow,' Lucy called out. 'Thanks love, I am sure you will make a superb father.'

'Hmm, Superb?' Bow asked with pessimism. 'I pray I don't disappoint you.'

The real issue wasn't whether he had the potentials to be a good father; it was whether he had the zeal to shepherd another man's cubs. He could adopt his business, have his wife but his children? That was a little hard to swallow.

'What's running through my darling's mind?'

Bow smiled and swam towards her as he searched for an appropriate response.

'I was just wondering how much longer I would have to wait before you become totally mine,' he giggled into her ears.

Lucy felt his tongue brushing her ears. It was ecstatic.

'Almost everything is set, my dear.' She hesitated and turned to face him. 'We can't afford to strike twice. One decisive blow and-'

She kissed him long and hungrily.

This moment, there were no butterflies in Bow's tummy. His thoughts were crystal clear as he recounted how deep the whole scheme had now run; an error too good to dismiss.

Most of Stephen's treasured files were already abducted, secured in his cabinet and although Stephen was yet to smell a rat, the meal was almost cooked.

'I've double inspected every bolt to the plan,' Bow reassured her. 'It's your signal that's restraining me.'

'Can't stop trusting you,' Lucy confessed splashing some water on him.

Bow grunted and crawled out of the pool. 'Darling please if you don't mind my asking, what will become of Julie's boy?' He would have called him by name if he remembered the name.

Lucy exhaled deeply. 'That's something that has been bothering me. I have been trying to make it a domestic issue but my options are few. What's your own opinion?'

Bow didn't need to hear all these. He had a premonition it would get to this. What was he getting himself into? Becoming a baby mop?

'Sincerely speaking,' he replied after he didn't hear Lucy's voice. 'We may have to explore other options. The most important thing is that he remains okay.'

Lucy raised her eyebrows.

'We currently have enough issues on our hands,' Bow declared jumpily. 'Some things can sort themselves out- with time,' he added.

Lucy calmly nodded and crept out after him.

The voices were torturing him. He pressed his ear against the cell bar but they were raising and dropping it at will. This was the second time in five days that his matter was being discussed to his hearing. The only other time, the voices were angry, loud and assaultive. He immediately had recognised the voices. Otima was the masculine vexed voice- calling him names from out of view and eventually coming to the cell to throw threats at him. He had never seen him in this mood- of course he had never had cause to. But he seemed like a man who hadn't lost his cool in a very long while. His tantrums were very mechanical and his choice of words would have evoked Stephen's laughter on another day.

He had come dressed in a short sleeved shirt and an over-the belly trouser with crossover belts- the cute picture of a retired headmaster. Even that apparel mocked the intents of his visit but he had communicated to the point that the police officers on duty had transformed gradually from sympathy to caution. He threw threats at will- even promised Stephen that he would engage the witch doctors to eliminate him. At that point, the uniformed men had to intervene. Stephen had made an initial attempt to explain to him but the man was justifiably pissed.

Enema on her own part wailed aloud, praying Julie to come avenge her death. It was not a spectacle the Police Headquarters was used to. They tried pleading their voices down to no avail, then coercion. Even that made the woman more agitated.

She turned on her dirges, attacking both Stephen and the policemen for conspiring to kill her daughter. The songs begged the officers to kill her too. Though she sang in their dialect, people could always tell a mournful song from a pop.

Stephen pressed his ear harder, it slid through the bars and was conveniently stuck between the bars. He wanted to more of the conversations Lucy was having with the inspector and the more they tuned their voices down, the higher his curiosity rose. By his inherent timing, their negotiation was taking forever.

After five nights, he had begun to look scruffy. Just before the negotiations began, Lucy had come over to whisper elaborately to him the terms of his captivity. She explained how she had been trying to garner resources to secure his bail and how they- she, Bow and a strange Lawyer she had secured his services had gone to court to activate the bail clause for his sake. Joe- the trusted Avri lawyer was yet to return from his vacation. The stories seemed to tie up. Stephen kept on mumbling thank you. In all of her narration, she didn't mention Julie's parents and how strong their prosecution team was. Stephen knew she was purposefully keeping that joker apart. He preferred it one rung at a time.

He trusted her to secure his bail- not like he had any other choice- and after the infra-tonic conversations, the voices became quite audible. This was the part they wanted him to hear.

'Honestly, I'm just doing this because you have given us a reason to trust you. On no account should this man run away o.'

'No he won't,' she reassured. 'Shebi I have surrendered his travelling documents to you?'

'You know criminals have their way of sneaking out.'

'Don't you dare call my husband a criminal!' Lucy shouted at the Inspector.

Stephen was impressed.

'He's lucky to have a persevering wife like you,' the unrepentant officer added. 'Please, better be careful with him.'

As he said that, he ordered that Stephen be released. Stephen stood there watching Lucy sign the last of the bail papers. He wondered if Otima knew about this at all.

'Mr Man, better be careful where you go and you are to report to this station every day.'

Stephen nodded and read off the name tag on his breast. A.Y Rizi. It was the same officer that had accosted him in his house five days ago. There was a trace of malice in his dictation. He was staring foolishly at Lucy too.

He greeted the Inspector and then Lucy. Both didn't seem a bit interested. She instead re-evaluated the husband that was left in him; just these few days and he looked this morose.

She led the way to her car; dropping tips to a couple of officers who hailed 'Madam'. Rizi followed Lucy closely behind like an ADC. Stephen wondered whether the Police had thought it safe to give her one- in case he was a serial killer on the prowl.

Rizi stopped three feet short of the car. Stephen gave him a disdainful stare and climbed into the passenger side.

Police men. They were a scornful lot.

Enema cast a knowing glance at her husband. Her eyes were very heavy and the nights of tearful wakefulness were beginning to tell on her. It was her opinion that they come see Fr.Thomas- the parish priest- who knew their story. The priest had naturalized into one of them after over two decades of staying in Ikeozi. He knew Julie very well- she had been one of the helping hands in his parsonage. She had been young, pro-active and ever willing to serve.

He had been stunned when news filtered in of her death but he was not the type to respond first-hand to rumours. It hurt him deeply because in the last three visits, she had always found the time to stop over and bless his holiness and he in turn would pray for her.

His fears had been confirmed when he woke up to meet her parents in his waiting room.

Enema had burst out in tears as he stepped in.

'Father, what have we done to deserve this?'

He was shaken but he tried not to cry too as he moved over to console her. He knew his white cassock wasn't going to pull through the exercise unstained but he just had to do that. Enema wailed and sobbed until Otima intervened.

'Enema, please shut up,' he reproved. 'We came here for something. Please let's get to it.'

Fr. Thomas pleaded with his eyes that he shouldn't aggravate his wife. After another twenty minutes, she managed to calm down.

In that twenty minutes, Otima shut his eyes again and imagined where

To Err is Woman

he was heading next. He knew the answers he sought would never be found in church. He had only come to fulfil all righteousness before he would go to the solution centre. Enema had pressed on him that they should seek the Priest's opinion and he had only agreed early this morning.

Now he just had to stand the consolatory romances this bachelor was rendering his wife. It was not the man's fault- celibacy vows had sleek exemptions. He would let the man steal some currents for another fifteen minutes, he concluded.

Something usually happened before the deadline. Enema stopped sobbing in the nick of time and he had the Priest's attention for the first time.

Otima wished his wife would do the narration. He wasn't keen to tell stories to someone he was sure wouldn't help any bit. Since Enema was not in the best spirits to talk, he began his tale.

Fr. Anthony's countenance didn't alter any bit. It was either he wasn't listening or he was splendid in concealing emotions. Otima had only finished explaining how Lucy had taken the risk of coming to inform them of Julie's death when Fr. Anthony interrupted him.

'Please, let me get her some water to drink,' he said pointing at Enema. He stood up and walked to his kitchen. Enema was stunned at the bold gender-bias that he was exhibiting. The drink was necessary although. At least, it would clear her throat to continue with the story. He could swear that Men of God loved drama and Enema had become nothing less than dramatic since the tragedy. It was an experience that spontaneously reversed their long standing roles in the family. He had become the man again- decisive and a beacon for a very volatile wife. For him, the ultimate test of his manhood would be his ability to bring Stephen to justice and how soon.

The Priest returned with his glassful of water and served Enema. There was none for Otima, after all he didn't cry out. His badly soiled gown was starting to irritate him. He had zero tolerance for dirt but he had to keep wearing this. He wasn't sure the tears had permanently stopped.

After Enema had taken three small gulps, Otima gently asked her to continue the story while he observed Fr. Anthony's face.

Her tone was all the more empathic for the full hour she spoke. Though she did not break down in tears again, the sadness was so transparent that Otima thought he saw tears hiding in the Priest's eyes.

He sniffed under his breath. He ought not have come here to reap tears from another man. He had his own store-full of tears.

'Bless God.' Father Anthony began. None of them bothered to respond with the trademark 'Forever more'. Obviously they saw no reason to bless God.

'Indeed, I am deeply touched by the reality of what began as a mere rumour.' He was selecting his words with caution. 'Julie was a lovely kid and an even more lovely woman.'

Enema nodded. 'It pains me to think that the sons of men would go this mile to kill another of God's creation.'

'We are not talking about sons of men. Just one son,' Otima rudely corrected.

'Really, Julie never for once complained of any frostiness in her home,' Fr Anthony continued. 'And I asked her always,' he added.

'Nor to me,' Enema quipped. 'That is where it hurts me much.'

Otima didn't like this show of sympathy. His plans were made. He was tackling Stephen head-long.

'God will help us. It is only he who knows the heart of men.'

'Father, my husband is very bitter. I am afraid for what he may do.'

Otima was shocked. Enema had ensnared him to come report him to the priest. That wasn't part of their mission.

'Who wouldn't be?' He turned to Otima. 'Vengeance is of the Lord Daddy.'

Otima hissed. What else would he say? Had he ever fathered a real child, watched her grow and then suddenly realize that she had been slain by a named assailant?

He didn't blame the priest. He judged as his limitations dictated.

Fr. Anthony had taken them through a biblical collection of people who had seen adversity and how their responses had affected the outcome. Job was the usual reference yet very few people named their children after him. Why wasn't he Fr. Job instead. He endured his sermon until the sun came out. By then, Enema was sleeping on the arm of the sofa, her exhausted snores reminding his husband that what had to be done was to be done. He had fulfilled this righteousness. His answers were way beyond the tabernacle of Fr. Anthony's god.

'Zwitt baby.'

The soft alluring voice made him stir and turn to the direction of the call. His eyes were still tight shut. It was very early in the morning and the recent peace that heralded the Avris seemed to have made it into the morning.

Lucy sat by Zwitt's pillow, her hands stroking his sleepy face.

'Wakie wakie my little Prince.'

Zwitt recognized the voice alas. The same words had woken him up for three consecutive dawns and the aberration was starting to get familiar.

Lucy was gradually becoming his mother.

The 'little Prince' sat up and rubbed the sleep glue off his eyelids.

He smiled at Lucy and muttered, 'Mommy Good morning.'

Lucy smiled back at him. 'How was your night?'

'It was good,' he replied glancing at the windows. He hadn't brought down his curtains before he slept so he could see beyond the room. It was still dark outside. He didn't feel he had slept for long and he craved for more sleep.

Things had eased up significantly since that outing he had with his father.

'It's not yet morning dear,' Lucy confirmed. 'I want you to keep these things until I demand for them.'

She handed him an enveloped package. 'I'll most likely need them later today.'

Zwitt nodded, collected the item and placed it aside his pillow.

'Common, don't be careless with that.' Her voice tensed up a tiny bit.

She retrieved it and tucked it underneath his pillow.

The pillow bulged under the discomforting pressure. Zwitt shot her a peek. She saw the bulge and flashed him a 'Just manage it' smirk.

At least he was grateful she was entrusting responsibilities on him. It was a remarkable improvement.

'You can still dig out few hours of sleep if you shut those lovely eyes now,' she finished closing his eyes with her palms. Lucy rose to leave as Zwitt settled back into sleep. He really needed that.

School run time. Zwitt, George and their kid sister- Geria sat in their sparkling uniforms- in the sitting room and waited for their father to emerge.

It was Wednesday and Stephen Avri held the unflinching responsibility of driving his kids to school every mid-week. He had arisen a little later than he was supposed to but he knew how to step up his morning rituals. He was confident that the children would meet the Early morning Assembly.

Zwitt checked Geria's school bag, the water bottle was inside. Her lunch snacks were toasted bread and caprisonne on Wednesday and she had hid them on the side pouch away from the cold drizzles that would eventually emanate from the water bottle. Her books were in a separate compartment and he double-checked for her assignments. They were all en-suite.

Having waited a while, Geria slid off the sofa and playfully dressed down Zwitt's stockings. He bent over and they began a rhythmic wind up and down stockings game. Geria hopped from one leg to the other as Zwitt labored to arrest her. They could do anything to kill their dad's delay.

To Err is Woman

Inside the master bedroom, Stephen put the final touches on himself, put on his tie and strode back to the mirror for the third and last time. Queer as it was, all his ties had been permanently knot by Julie perhaps because he never had the finesse to knot one accurately and because Lucy had no interest in his outlook- a strident contrast to Julie.

He was meticulous when it came to fashion- his apparel strictly matched the occasion. When the going was good, he spent an hour every night roaming through his wardrobe, selecting and rejecting choices until he made a perfect pick for the next day. The stray compliments he usually earned encouraged his attitude.

This morning, he was somehow in that mood. He stepped his impeccable body back from the mirror and stooped to pick the car keys. He couldn't take his eyes off the mirror. His fingers felt nothing. He pulled the drawers three-quarter out and wiped his palm across the inside. It was stark empty.

Stephen frowned into the mirror. He did still look handsome in spite of the frown. His car keys had never been any other place but here. This was a first.

'Lucy,' he called out popping his head into her room. 'Have you got the keys?'

'What keys?' She spun around in cosmetic surprise. She walked into his room.

'The car keys of course.' Lucy's room was a subset of her husband's own, aside the door, the partitioning glass was transparent from both ends. 'All the car keys are gone,' Stephen reiterated.

'Are you sure darling?'

Stephen didn't acknowledge the darling that he had suddenly become. They hadn't shared such novelties this week at least. He nodded. 'Those keys have never slept outside that drawer.'

Lucy didn't need to go check the drawer. He had disengaged it and it lay independently on the floor. She then tried to mope around the chest in case the keys had climbed out to hide elsewhere.

'Have you asked the kids?'

'Not yet.' He stormed out. 'Where are the car keys,' he yelled as he entered the sitting room.

Geria's hands retracted from Zwitt's leg, terrified at her father's fury. 'Zwitt!'

He shook his head innocently. Lucy stepped in, her eyes prowling.

'Go and get those keys!'

Zwitt was confused. He looked on.

All four pair of eyes were on him. He felt like he could feel his own eyes penetrating himself as well.

'Idiot, go and get those things,' Lucy bellowed decisively.

Zwitt shuddered and dragged his feet to his room. Almost everyone followed closely behind. It was only Geria that stayed back. Zwitt was in deep trouble and she couldn't stand the sight of what might happen to him next.

As Zwitt shuffled to his room, his heart skipped. When Lucy talked about 'those things', he clearly understood but not when she talked about 'car keys'. He had nothing on car keys. Inside the room, he retrieved a wrapped up item from under the pillow. Stephen had already heard the clicking of keys but he urged himself to open it.

Indeed, they were his keys that the domestic miscreant had wrapped up. Lucy quickly took charge.

'Sweetheart, we are very lucky that he started with keys o and not–'

'Who told you that's all he has robbed?' He found his voice. 'We just nipped him in the bud.' He made a 'I hope so' face. 'Those keys could have landed in the wrong hands.' He was shouting at the top of his voice.

Stephen examined one of the bunches. 'Gosh, that's the key to my contract box!' He was mad. 'How did he get to this? We have a witch in the house.'

'God,' Lucy was even more dramatic. 'Zwitt you will not kill me in this house.'

Stephen stared at his first son in bitter realization. There was no hint of remorse on his face. He was instead staring back at all of them- a hardened criminal's poise.

He selected another key. 'Lucy please take G and G to school.' He handed the key to her and turned to Zwitt. 'Get into my car!'

Five minutes later, Zwitt sat on a portion of the rear seat and wondered what precisely he had done wrong. So many ugly words had been traded all off a sudden and the only fact he was certain of was that school had been cancelled for him today.

'Zwitt, where is Daddy taking you to?' George's contrite face appeared by the door. He seemed very scared.

Zwitt fought back the tears and shook his head. 'Please just help me tell Miss Sowofa I can't be in school today.'

George nodded feebly as Stephen climbed behind the wheels.

'Dad, where are you taking Zwitt to?' George was not satisfied.

Stephen pondered on the perfect response as he selected his gear.

'Home,' he said as he drove away.

'I want him killed,' Otima bellowed. 'Just the same way he slew my Julie.'

Ezedum stared hard at the piece of cloth in his hand. It was a mangled stripe cut from a tie. This was Otima's second visit and he was still as agitated as ever. This time he had come unaccompanied probably as a show of resilience.

Ezedum knew he was going to return. He had read his mind and seen that irrepressible cry for vengeance inside it. Three days ago, he had perceived a familiar footstep being trailed by a strange one as they trotted to his shrine. The formalities had given way to the reasons why foremost Christian revolutionist would sneak into his temple. It was just past dawn and it took about an hour for the fastest walkers to get to his shrine from

Ikeozi. Otima had been wise in his choice of accomplice- Seeki was a veteran in witch-hunting and diabolism. He obviously had talked Otima into this bid and even though the latter looked decisive, Ezedum wished he could spare this man the brutality ahead. Their demands had been complicated further by the god's insistence that Stephen's hands were clean.

The Chief Priest stared repeatedly at his pot, stirred it two more times than required but the stones continued to settle at odd points. He wasn't sure what to do next. He was a notorious priest but he had a reputation of hurting the wicked only. Otima's story had been pathetic. If he had fathered a daughter himself, he would not have hesitated to unleash terror on the perpetrator. His demands were expectedly terminal but his pot was saying otherwise. Ezedum had pensively decided to buy more time. He asked Otima to return in three days with a needless personal property from Stephen. In the time in between, he hoped that he would be able to think a line of action through.

Business had been on an all-time low, people were rebelling and turning to strange religions. They would rather go and sit piously in pews than confront what faced them squarely. His family was starting to feel the bite of his lack of income and just the night before, he had actually held a late night conversation with the wife on the prospects of making a U-turn to Christianity. The next day, the gods had sent him Otima- a church warden. And the same gods wouldn't indicate that his transgressor was guilty.

'Otima, your request is easy but…'. The 'but' was the hard part.

'I have come a long way. I have done as you demanded. Stephen has to dance to the same music he forced my daughter to dance.'

Ezedum made up his mind. He joggled three pebbles and put it before Otima. Let every man pick his destiny with his hands. The pebbles rested on defined creases on his palm. The most proximal crease on the hand of the Ancient one stood for truth. If Otima picked that, he would hear what he would not like. The second rested on the mid-transverse crease. It represented the prevalence of human will over the dictates of his god. The last pebble was interlocked between the ring and middle finger. It appeared trapped and would require deliberate effort to liberate it. It meant an extreme hunger for vengeance.

Otima studied all three stones. He had no idea why they were at different positions but he knew he needed fast results. It had hurt him more when he heard that Stephen had been granted bail even without his notification. He had lost all faith in the legal apparatus nor did he ever have any belief in the church's manner of retribution.

Ezedum wore his usual multi-colored raffia and sat on a tripod of skulls as huge billows of smoke proceeded from the shroud right behind him. His frigid personality was in sharp contrast to the intimidating sights that greeted unfamiliar visitors to the shrine. On his first visit, he hadn't bothered to glance around- they had only stated their case and watched the Priest do his incantations. Today, he was much more relaxed and his eyes had veered through every visible section of the shrine. There was fresh blood lining the whole circumference of the consulting room. They smelled like chicken blood and the presence of tufts of feathers also aided his judgement. The usual hides and leopard skin were hanging from some branches of the huge Oji tree that was the shrine. Its stem had been naturally burrowed into by the gods and it was inside it that Ezedum mantle reigned supreme.

'Pick one,' Ezedum urged.

Otima looked closely. He made his choice and dashed for the third pebble- the same that was stuck between two fingers. He probed for the pebble with the intent of a determined man and just as his fingers felt its surface, Ezedum parted his fingers and the content of his palm fell to the floor.

Otima looked up at him, 'Ezedum what was that for?'

Ezedum cleared his throat. He had not dropped the pebbles on purpose but Otima had unwittingly hurt his knuckles where he had sustained a nail puncture yester-night. Still, all were acts of the gods- no matter how the humans perceived them.

'Otima.' He called him as a man would call his peer. Not as the god's mouthpiece. 'Wives are like beans. Sometimes they come half-done, well-done or overdone. At times you eat them white or jollof..or with plantain or sweet potatoes. You may add stew on them and relish the taste with bread, pap or garri.'

Otima stared on. 'Wives are like beans?' he asked rhetorically. 'Ezedum, what has beans got to do with me?'

Ezedum shook his head. He didn't expect him to understand but truly he just made up his mind. There was no need to implicate himself any further.

'The man whose blood you desire is blameless before the gods.'
'No way!'
Both men stared at each other. Otima counted his remaining options.

Lucy screeched her car to a halt undisturbed by the dust she raised and the scuttling away of nearby school kids. She was uncommonly eager to be done with the school run. Her mind jammed and jerked all along probably because she was driving her kids to school on an unusual day! That was her; she could sincerely afford to stay deceptive even to herself.

She watched Geria lazily shuffle out of the car, her little school bag glued to her tiny fingers. Her gaze was firm on the ground as though it searched for some precious lost items. As she shut the door, Lucy pushed her door open.

'Geria.'

The little girl turned her head to the direction of the cal. Her eyes were heavy so she resolved to keep them on the floor. Lucy heaved wondering how best to dissipate the tension. In spite of herself, she truly loved her children- her children.

'Geria,' she whispered. 'You won't give Mom a goodbye kiss?'

The kiss wasn't routine but it was a strategy she employed occasionally when emotions ran deep. Her daughter was overtly emotional- an unsafe poise for an eventual lady in the world. She prayed the appeal would take.

Lucy chuckled as her little baby clumsily went round the car to her own side. She stopped few inches from her face.

Lucy stylishly turned her cheeks in anticipation. She didn't see Geria muster up some saliva.

A paste of sputum hit her cheeks. She was taken aback. She made to grab her but she had already jumped beyond her reach.

'Goodbye mum,' she screamed suddenly rediscovering her excitement. She was very relieved by her feat.

Lucy mopped up the spit on her face and watched her dart towards her classroom. Her own child dare not contest her authority.

Nemesis rang loud in her head. She shook her head violently in refute. It could not be. It was certainly a subtle show of infantile delinquency but she had to curb it quick and decisively.

She leaned against the steering, drained of any next-line of action. It was her own stroke of luck that she had dropped George before Geria or the interpretation would have been altered.

One thing was clear; She had work to do.

12

'Faro was the boy of the present. An older than he looked obstinate twelve year old with an awful self-impression of wit and doughtiness. Over the years, he had carved out a niche that he gave all he had to sustain.

His other name was Terror- an apt referral to the fear he aroused among his peers. He was really not that aversive but Faro would not as much as sneeze without finding someone to punch for causing him 'to react to him.' Those with a little discretion kept their distance from him but he had the inept ability to draw close- suddenly.

So far, his story was simple and he repeatedly told it in solemn terms to anyone who gave his ears. He had been born Chinonye Ofaro to a Somalian refugee who had found his way into Nigeria and then into his mother's pants. At three years, he already had the notion that the only night his parents had agreed on any point must have been on the day he was conceived. The rebellious man did nothing to ease the panic and discrimination his wife faced for marrying a man without a traceable history. Really, they were not married- they simply lived together after she took in. Faro had grown up christened after his mother's name. The young Chino- as the mother called him-

was forced to grow up without a father. The Somalian had fled- probably to re-join his militant group when he was just four and all the innocent questions he asked his mother as he grew up often elicited cruel answers. At seven, he was prudent enough to stop asking. In his loneliest moments, he sought for hints of good words to describe his father with. He was never successful at that. His mother tried her best to nudge him on but she could only stay eight months after the man who ruined her life fled. She died a heart broken woman.

The images never dimmed; the transaction between his maternal aunt and Miss Neho. The latter was as poor as she was indifferent. That bargain was the trough of his life but he had long moved on.

Today, he was nothing less than a celebrity. He was the Lord of the Little Angels. Even that status hadn't come easy. There had been lots of compromising and Blackmailing- an Art Faro was perfecting by the day.

Once, he had extorted another inmates box camera and had embarked on a snapping spree in the Home. What started out as a motive-free venture eventually yielded the weapon with which he exerted his dominance.

The apparent healthy relationship that existed between the old squeaky matron and her much younger deputy- Ben Awo had been demystified by Bow's adventurous spirits. He had been the first to notice slight lapses in visual exchanges between the duo and he had pursued his suspicion.

Ben had been married without kids for a while and his mistress- Neho was just on the brink of menopause- she too unfortunately a spinster. Her hormonal profile was still normal and she was experiencing the last surge of the sexual hormones. It was logically permissible that they indulged in each other since there was minimal risk of procreation- in any case.

Ben however knew he had his marriage to protect. He wasn't the only one who knew there was something at stake. Faro also did. He was fed up with gossips so he went for the jugular; evidences no one could debunk.

Three rapid flashes unnoticed by the excited bodies in the dark and he had his most-priced possession. That was the price he had to pay to become the Lord.

Two days later, he made a couple of other inmates privy to the elaborate secret and as the pictures passed from row to row in the dining-hall, the kids made faces and laughed in styles.

In another twelve hours, Faro was summoned to the Matron's office; this time not for questioning but for negotiations. Nobody had ever had it that cosy at Little Angels.

At an undisclosed cost, he took his oath of secrecy and handed over some of the pictures. There was however one dramatic change after that; Faro was always right. His rank grew spontaneously but as they say- Change never ends.

The euphoria had long ebbed away.

CeeCee doled out food into the last of the empty bowls, sized up the left over in the huge pot and blew her whistle. The array of plates began to disappear erratically, plucked by tiny sets of hands whose faces underlined their appetites. Lunch was being served at 4p.m- just twenty minutes behind schedule but they were all expediently hungry.

They were always hungry, CeeCee thought to herself. *And a little extra starvation shouldn't really mean much to their customarily empty stomachs.* She had suggested that the kids be dewormed but the Matron had ignored her opinion.

In an orphanage where she doubled as both the cook and the dining-mistress, all her beneficiaries were careful not to be enlisted in her black book. The consequences were usually dire.

The frenzy of the bowl-run had given way to the extremely irritating sight of poorly bred children displaying all odd forms of table manners- *table dismanners*, she often called it.

She cast her glance on the serving table. One plate was still unclaimed as it lay coyly beside her massive pot.

Who could that be? She had done a head count before she dished out the food. Who hadn't come forward? She grazed from one end of the hall to the other. There were over a hundred kids, adorned in same uniform and without much ado squeezed into the small refectory. From her position, she couldn't tell who had which plates- besides a handful of the kids opted to eat from the plates on their hands.

Someone was marching towards her- slowly but surely. Then it struck her. Faro! He had been brewing this problem for some time. The night before, he had had the rare boldness to request for an extra ration. Of course, CeeCee turned him down.

As Faro marched up to her, his eyes were blind to the huge stern figure that was CeeCee nor was he seeing the tiny bowl that held the miserable food that should have been his. His entire mind was set on the remnants in the pot- remnants that surpassed over a quart of the entire meal. He had patiently waited for her to notice that a plate was unclaimed and the moment she did, he had swung into action. This woman had unapologetically stepped on his toes and he had always excused her.

Today was Judgement Day.

CeeCee was thinking in like rein. She had long anticipated a show-down with the brute but now that it was imminent, she couldn't tell whether she was prepared. Her instincts told her to take the first blow. As Faro drew much closer, she smiled contemptuously and then withdrew some portions from the bowl. If Faro thought his ration was small, she made it smaller.

Faro ignored her. He approached the table, stood on his toes and took a long greedy peep into the pot. An ocean of saliva filled his mouth. CeeCee reserved more than she shared.

'Take your food and get out of here,' CeeCee roared. She had the attention of the few who hadn't noticed the brewing confrontation.

'My food?' Faro's smirk gave her palpitations.

'I must take you in this time!' she threatened. 'Enough is enough. Miss Dipo must do something about this.' There was less conviction in the latter threat. Everyone knew that Faro had immunity.

Faro nodded in consent, 'Of course, she shall.' He grabbed his bowl and emptied it inside the pot. He had to stretch to achieve that.

CeeCee watched alongside others in suspence.

'Today,' Faro announced impudently. 'Faro will eat from the pot.' He swooped the pot to himself. CeeCee almost lost her balance as she made a feeble attempt to reclaim the pot. A ripple of laughter swept through the hall.

'Are you hungry?'

CeeCee was too started to respond. Faro doled out a tired ration into the blank plate and shoved it at her. She surprisingly accepted the offer. She had no clue what was going to happen to the remaining food and she was indeed starving too.

She had not only disappointed herself, she had deprived her family of lunch and dinner. She had no clues that Faro's attack would be of this nature. She watched him from the corner of her eyes as she made a round across the tables- dishing extra portions into needy plates. After the generous effort, she sat down at a safe distance and devoured the rest.

Repercussions could come later. He wasn't bothered in any way.

Stephen sped down the route he had only had cause to ply just once. He knew each turn by heart and he negotiated the bends carefully. There was deafening silence inside his BMW.

He thought better about the silence and with a heavy touch, he put on the car stereo.

It was Abba's 'knowing me, knowing you' on air and for the first time in numerous years, he listened to the lyrics- hoping that they would not antagonize his mood.

Oops, he thought. There were just perfect. By the third refrain, he gladly sang along.

'Breaking up is never easy I know-'

For emphasis sake, he repeated that line once more than the artistes- perhaps to make Zwitt take it in; if he had such abilities.

'But I have to go,' he sang on. Indeed he had to. Much of his conquests had come from spontaneous breath-taking decisions. His instincts barely deceived him- they wouldn't start now.

taking decisions. His instincts barely deceived him- they wouldn't start now.

Stephen pictured the huge slab placed across the road. It had a 'Slow Down. Men at Work' inscription on it. The road was already a bit bumpy. He eased off his foot from the throttle as he appeared the recently damaged road. Nigerian roads could get bad overnight- once the witches plied the road. He pondered on how this road had become this bad in a space of few weeks.

His attention caught the huge J written on a recrudescent sign-post. His mystery was solved.

Jukotex Contractors was the State Government's authorized placebo on road maintenance and reconstruction. They had the reputation of breaking up fair roads and then spending ample time and of course- tax payers' money on the rejuvenation.

Government versus the people, ripping off the people and flogging the people- Demonic craze.

At about the same time, Stephen noticed that his song had stopped and the presenter was starting to blab. He resisted the urge to quickly change the dial and hoped that the husky voice would give way to some favourite tunes soon.

He shot Zwitt a quick glance from the over-head mirror. The poor boy sat motionless by the door, in the same manner that he had been when they set out. His belongings were firmly clutched to his belly.

Zwitt saw the lightening-speed glance from his father and summoned more courage.

Think up something, tell him something. He is your father for crying out loud. He chided himself. Sadly no sound idea came across his mind.

Still, anything was better than muteness. He resolved to give it a go.

'Dads,' Zwitt Avri began.

Stephen spun his face towards the kid with a stare that was supposed to stun him to ice. His resolve was strong.

'Why can't you love me?'

Avri sniffed and jammed on his brakes jolting Zwitt temporarily.

'You want to know?' he asked coldly. 'Why?'

He watched Zwitt's slow nods. At that instant, a million profane reasons sprang up.

'Because you are a bunch of creeping demons. Because you are not by any means worthy.' He paused. 'Because I am not sure you are my son.'

He stopped. How could he have said the last one? Julie was undoubtedly faithful to him.

Stephen swallowed his spit and with his right hand, he drew Zwitt's left ear close.

'Listen,' he started. 'I don't wish to hear more than one voice at a time in here and right now-' He turned up the stereo's volume with the left hand. '-I think this voice is more than sufficient.' He pulled it harder. 'Do you understand?'

Zwitt shook his head in pain, escaping Stephen's grip.

'Daddy, please.'

'Shut up.' The scream froze him up.

'I swear to God, if you make one more sound, I will gag you to death.'

He wasn't faking it. He was provoked- quite easily, he admitted to himself. That was unusual especially coming from him to a minor. What was going wrong with him? The pressure was starting to tell. The pressure of having harboured a notorious son until today.

Zwitt nodded. At least he had made an effort to talk to his father. He understood the threat but not the fury. All the same, he returned to his dumbness as Stephen re-geared the car into motion.

Myth Number One; Time flies. Certainly not tonight. Zwitt listened to every tick of his mind-clock, glancing in between moments at the nearest window with the anticipation of dawn. It seemed like seven nights had been squeezed into this night. He was certain he was the only awake person in the densely populated room as he stirred and wondered how his colleagues had managed to find sleep in these harsh conditions.

Croo croo. The invisible frogs came again with their disgusting sounds. He had only read in books that frogs croaked. He had never seen one nor heard the sound live. It was his neighbour who noticed his uneasiness and had explained to him.

'That's mbala,' he told him. The boy had gone the extra intimate mile of naming them by their croaks. 'He is the chief frog.' Zwitt nodded, his eyes lit up in bemusement. The boy took him on a quick lecture as more croaks came. Zwitt didn't wish to know that much about frogs and toads. He didn't ask him questions. The teacher understood and kept his wisdom to himself soon after.

There were a few hisses and rattling sounds too. They could be snakes- he had briefly watched some documentary about snakes on National Geographic and those sounds were familiar. He subconsciously calculated what chances he stood if any of the snakes crept in. He had a fair chance. His mat was in the centre of the pack-Unless the snakes hopped like frogs.

What had he signed into? A wave of hisses swept across the room punctuating the snores. Zwitt was used to it; there was a competitive spirit in the household. They often did things in rows and batches. When they snored, it was in rhythms and frequencies that bid to outdo the preceding one. Zwitt added his hiss. He wasn't letting up the flow. Lucy often said that 'If you must hiss, you better make it long.' The sound reverberated across breaking the sequence of snores. He heard people murmur at the other end.

Zwitt rubbed his eyes and tried to turn his neck.

'Arggh,' he cried. He just sprained his neck. He managed to get up, supporting himself with his left hand. It hurt him deeply. The mats were designed to be shorter than the occupants and apposed closely to the next ones. As a result, he had had to crawl up to prevent marching on the person right at his feet. Many of them slept like that and it was a mystery how they maintained that poise even while asleep.

The sleeping hall had indiscrete carton partitions and even the dusty cartons were enough to unleash status asthmaticus on pre-disposed persons.

Section D was for fresh-men and progression to better sections depended on new entries and new ones were sparse to see. He had no idea how long his stay in Section D would last.

His thoughts reeled back to the events of yesterday. His dad had removed the unnecessary gag from his mouth as they approached the new home. He hadn't bothered to re-wear the tie- he just simply flung it unto the empty seat beside him. Zwitt had watched him with sworn dumbness.

Stephen seized his hand and literally dragged him into the Matron's office. She was a curious figure- a bizarre picture.

'Hey. See whom we've got here.' She muttered a little loudly. 'Mr Avri, you finally made it.'

Zwitt's surprise was brief. He looked up to catch the smirk on Stephen's face.

'I must admit that it had to be,' Stephen replied sitting down without invitation. 'Though not as soon as we had thought.'

'Justice may be delayed but never-' She couldn't complete even the commonest of quotes. Her eyes pranced about as she hoped the missing word would just filter in.

'Denied,' Stephen helped her.

Crooks, Zwitt thought. *So they had hatched the idea for quite a while and they weren't wasting time to disclose that.*

'You know it's been quite a while since you visited,' she frowned to herself. 'Things are not the way you met them then.'

Stephen maintained his expressionless face.

'We've had real threatening times,' Neho pressed on. 'The facility is filled beyond its brim and even adding a toy would be suicidal.'

Zwitt watched Stephen fumble for a while for something in his pocket and then his hand re-emerged with his cheque booklet.

Neho's countenance changed instantly.

'We can however work out something.' Her eyes were stuck on his cheque booklet. 'We can work out a space,' she repeated in case Stephen didn't hear at first.

'In whose favour should i-' Stephen was on the current leaf, about to write.

'Neho Dipo,' she quickly enthused. *How could he ask or almost ask that question?*

'Sir,' she began. 'We ought to work out a partnership- some form of standing agreement.'

Neho studied Zwitt for a minute. The latter met her gaze briefly and then let it drop.

'You've got yourself a very shy boy, Mr emm emm.' She cleared her throat for suddenly forgetting Stephen's name. 'Handsome,' she resumed rubbing Zwitt's head. 'please, can you wait for us outside?'

Zwitt nodded and stepped out.

He was re-invited into the office after thirty minutes for the final rituals of their transaction.

Stephen patted him on the back and said 'See you soon Son.'

A second strange woman came and led him away. He wouldn't lift his face to stare Stephen on the face. Stephen on his own part completely ignored the tears that splattered on the floor. Growing up was never really easy.

The moment the door shut behind him, he sucked up the tears. His tour-guide was another effective creation of error. Her chubby cheeks and very unserious eyes eased up Zwitt's spirits a little. She had a height that by no means matched the deposits of fats she was endowed with. She was tactically a dwarf.

Zwitt hissed the memories away and got up. As he glided away, he avoided the several figures on the floor. The sparse light from the half-shut door guided his steps. Two shoves at the door and he realised that they had been jailed in the room. He traced the chains to a padlock. They were prisoners at night. He hissed in disgust. He had hoped he could get some fresh air outside. He turned around and walked back to his space. Halfway back, he was suddenly tripped by an outstretched leg. He could have sworn the path was clear before he placed his own legs. His face fell just in line with that of his detractor and the latter pegged him immediately to the floor with his arms.

'Let me go,' Zwitt said between his teeth.

'Zwitt.' He was surprised then he remembered that he had been introduced to everyone over dinner. He didn't answer.

'Let me off,' he fiercely protested. ' I'm going to scream.'

'Scream if you suppose that will save you,' the voice bullied. Faro pressed his face on Zwitt's as if he was understudying some latent features.

'You are not as stupid as you look. Are you?'

Zwitt sniffed humid air into his face. That made him back off and sit up- hugging his knees as he sat.

Zwitt quickly stood up and examined him. His massive face was beat like a shrunken overripe orange and in spite of the lack of visibility, Zwitt was certain he could see rows of pimples across the ugly face.

'What's your problem?' Faro asked as he noticed the displeasure.

'I should be asking you that,' Zwitt retorted.

Faro stood up to him, hoping his bulky frame would do the usual trick. Zwitt scowled at the fabricated features especially the dangling lower lip. He hadn't seen that before now.

Faro cleared his throat rudely and loudly.

'You don't seem to get it? Do you?'

'Get what?' Zwitt asked irritably.

'That if you are not for me, there is no future for you.'

Zwitt scowled deeper. 'Who are you?'

'Fa-,' then he changed his mind. This brat couldn't dictate what he did or said.

'You will find out- sooner or later,' he replied instead.

'If I wish to,' Zwitt finished moving away.

Faro followed him briefly resisting the urge to draw him back.

'Don't ever try proving tough,' he warned. 'You will never find it easy.'

'Big mouth save your yak.' Zwitt wasn't sure he knew what 'yak' meant but Lucy used to use it repeatedly.

'You think you've got a sharp tongue?' Faro shouted back. 'You will drown fast and surely.' He didn't give a hoot who his scream awoke.

Zwitt opted to ignore him this time as he laid down again on his mat. Adversity was something that came naturally to him.

As Faro walked back to his cubicle, his confidence waivered a little. Collins, Femi, Jimmy and Atu, all started tough. Then he had tamed them. Yet there was this intrinsic strength Zwitt had. He hadn't seen its equivalent. Time would tell.

As the saliva drooled off his mouth unto the hard desk, Stephen opened his eyes-slowly at first and then with some panic. He checked the time. 5a.m. To think that he had been snoring under such harsh conditions made his shiver.

He stood up and stretched then he sat on his desk- making sure he wiped the splash of saliva on the table with his butts. He was turning rapidly into something else.

He remembered his secretary bidding him good bye at about 5pm the previous day. Even Jereny had atypically shown his face as he left the building. He had responded to both like one work-encumbered bull, had hardly raised his face even to acknowledge them. He had a heap of files to the left of his desk and about three top priority ones right in front of him but they really didn't match the enthusiasm he was investing on them. Those were things he could sort out with his regular pace.

Deep down, his cravings were clear. He wanted to hear his phone ring at some point and then he would listen to Lucy's pleaful voice asking what was keeping him out late. He longed to detect in her voice; that utter loneliness a woman felt in the absence of her man.

Time passed and nothing happened.

At 11pm, he had heaved in disgust and persuaded himself to be a bit more patient. Lucy had apparently dozed off in her wait and would soon wake up with a start.

Instead, he was the one that woke with a start. There were no missed calls on his phone- just annoying bulk messages sent by his network providers. The cleaners were starting to come to work and he could hear some exchanges of pleasantries downstairs. He straightened up his jackets, picked a few files and left the office.

The abrupt silence that greeted his descent from the stairs told him the rest of the tale. These were workers who had hardly seen him in person.

The first to hear his footsteps had shifted safely away from the foot of the stairs.

'Who be that?' he shouted.

Stephen didn't bother to respond. The stairs were in spirals and as his leg came into view, the man mustered some courage to draw nearer.

He obviously didn't know who he was but at least he had the common sense to match the attire with an office.

'Oga, goodmorning.'

Stephen nodded and moved past.

It was outside the building that he got the warm reception he didn't need.

'Oga! You follow us work this night?' the gateman was being stupidly caring. 'Haba nah. You no need to de stress yourself like this nah.'

Stephen forced a smile as he drove out. He used to know that particular gateman's name.

Eight hours earlier. Lucy spontaneously pushed the pause button on the DVD remote and eyed her kids. From where she lay prone, she discerned

Geria's faint snores from George's slightly heavier moan- or snore. She smiled promiscuously as her eyes returned to the frozen nude bodies on the screen. The film was just halfway in and her whole body ached and yelled for a man. She was not sure she could continue this torture when she had an option- or options. She needed a real man to extinguish these flames from her polluted mind.

She arose to carry the kids into their rooms.

'But Mummy, i don't want to go inside.'

Lucy froze in her tracks. She had successfully laid Geria down on the bed and returned to carry George. His eyes were alert- he obviously hadn't slept a wink in the past hour.

The brat had fooled her.

'You want to do what then, eh George?' she shouted at him.

He didn't even hear. His eyes were fixed on the screen and the disappointment of an incomplete viewing showed on his face.

Lucy reached for the remote and pressed the off button. Now the entire room was completely dark.

Her cat eyes traced George's hand and she half-dragged him into the bedroom.

Silly boy, like his father.

She returned to the sitting room and spared some thoughts on why Stephen hadn't returned home nor called to explain.

Perhaps, he had enrolled into the Orphanage with Zwitt. She chuckled at the idea. After all, they were both orphans.

She shoved the lewd thought away. Since Stephen didn't feel the compulsion to call and explain, she was not going to waste time wondering what could have happened.

She got up from the sofa to fetch her phone.

The phone rang twice and Bow's drowsy voice sent some fire down her spine. This guy was just it.

She grinned. At least she knew one man who could be home- one real man.

'Hello Bow love,' her voice was wet.

'Lucy how now?' He was struggling to wake up.

His house was about five streets away- a distance Lucy could afford to walk. The only hindrance was that massive length of bare land that led out of her house and even more worrisome was the sharp division in neighbourhood between Bow's street and theirs. His street had a fair share of touts and night peddlers and if she was ever recognised, she stood a chance of being mobbed or blackmailed.

After opening exchanges, she landed.

'Bow darling, please can i come around?'

The whisper skipped through Bow's ears and down to his groin. He had an instant erection. This lady was never short of tricks.

'You want to?' he asked.

'Do you want me to?'

They started their trade of rhetoric like young school lovers would. She kept the line alive as she drove the eleven minutes route into his arms.

She never short changed her needs.

13

The last stack of books went down like he willed them. He simply had no clues and it was even hard to believe that he could have been this careless. Sulli never misplaced money- not to talk of almost a million naira. That was what his contracts represented- money tagged to faces.

He continued to flip rashly through the pages of the books he had already dislodged from the shelf- not because he believed any of them had the photograph but because he was never the one to give up. This was his fourth round of search.

He was pissed beyond words- all the more made worse by the fact that he could not share his frustration with anyone. The chilled room could not stop the sweats trickling between his buttocks and down the inside of his thighs.

He only had his boxers on and had turned the blades of the fan to face the shelf just to leverage the flip process through the books.

'I think you can now get to work.' Lucy's curt instruction rang in his head. He had dreamt and waited for same and eventually she had given him the go-ahead late this evening. He was surprised at his degree of confusion.

Sulli threw the last two books on the bed and sank in after them. His three hour long futile search had ruined the impeccability of his bedroom. It had also ruined what should have been an evening of celebration. He was oblivious of the figure at the other end of the end, tucked in under his blankets and following his every move with hurtful eyes begging to be incorporated.

The room was well lit and his eyes span across all ends. He was a man of order and precision. Everything had its position in his bedroom. The paper works had their corner; the books he assembled in the hope of eventually becoming a medical student upon quitting this calling, his clothes were divided between wardrobes- the clean and regular were always separated from the dirty ones. But all had definite hangers. He was obsessed with aseptic rules.

Why he had to fumble over what would have easily been his cheapest job unnerved him. He slapped through the first book and found nothing. He swore into it and threw it into the air. The leaves of the loosely bound book accepted his invitation to scatter all across the room. A couple settled on the arch of the inciting body on the bed.

The little idiots picture was not only denying him cash. If he failed to find it, Aswa's visit was certainly a waste of libido.

Aswa Totle struggled to overcome the urge to open her eyes to the light sensations greasing her brows. Her eyes had been shut for just about two minutes. She hoped it was Sulli's adventurous fingers but the feeling was too brittle and too fixed to be human. She narrowly opened her eyes. Paper! She hissed in her mind and shifted away from that caress. Her head ached with worries and ponders. She had laid on the bed for almost two hours waiting for the mysterious search to end. And Sulli's silence didn't help matters.

He called her about six hours ago requesting that she come over and in her usual handy manner, she showed up. She felt at home in his house and in her regular fashion, she had undressed and slid under the duvet. Perhaps if she had not got her mind on one thing, she would have observed the flinch that greeted her arrival and the growing uneasiness that followed every minute of searching. She didn't know this guy too well but she knew that he always received her well.

It had been three months today that they met and for friends that became lovers from day one, it was strange that in that span of time, the had had no reasons to argue over anything. This bothered Aswa. She had heard from her married friends that when couples had seamless peace, one of them was certainly a zombie in the union. She knew how stubborn she was as a lady and each time she re-evaluated the facts of their relationship, she saw nothing that she should have done differently. On another day, with another guy she would have boldly protested this attitude but instead, she saw herself making excuses for this guy. In the corners of her mind, she prayed she was not falling in love. And then she prayed again, that she was.

They had hooked up in the most unusual of circumstances- A disappointing evening that had by some miraculous stroke of fate become a blessed night. She remembered that stormy night- even the evening that ushered the night. She had sat out and watched the skies from her corridors. The sun had rested as early as 4pm and some thick clouds and strong winds gathered. She stared up repeatedly and wished that she had a husband or even a boyfriend of more permanent status. Then she made a decision. She was not going to bear this cold alone.

She put on her yellow mini skirt with her navel shy top and entered the wind. Her attire did all the explanations she needed to do and Bow in spite of a flagrant show of surprise and hesitation had welcomed her in.

They had begun a slow vain conversation on the three piece sofa and while Aswa enjoyed his fingers grazing on her hair, she wished they could fast-forward and get inside. Bow appeared uneasy on the night but she thought it was because she came unannounced. No man wanted to be bumped into indiscreetly. She saw reasons with him and even went further to apologise.

'I am sorry for just running into your place like this,' she had purred. 'I was literally freezing and i have no other person but you.'

Bow had nodded and put a finger on her lips. The apology was unnecessary and she was welcome.

The first bout of rain had just abetted and the heavens were roaring to unleash again. She had sat up and placed her head on his hairy chest while he kept fencing at the borders of her skirt. She could hear his heavy breaths and the rigidity of his penis gave her some hope. They would get there, she was damn sure.

Suddenly there had been a knock on his door. Aswa saw the panic in his eyes. She glanced at the clock. 9.33pm.

'Who on earth would be disturbing you by this time?'

She strained the disturbing.

Bow shook his head but his eyes betrayed him. This was why he had been jittery all along.

Without letting the intruder in, Bowono had helped both of them up.

'You have to do as I say,' he whispered taking her to the outlet door from the kitchen.

Within a minute and half, she was released into the fierce rain, armed with a disproportionate umbrella that only pretended to protect her.

She had walked only fifty metres and she was thoroughly soaked. The rain came in mocking fury. She shut the umbrella and slowed down. Did she always have to be second best?

Visibility was not easy but she was confident she could navigate.

'Cold?'

Aswa jumped just in time to feel the strong masculine arm rest on her shoulders and a roof of an umbrella come over her head.

She jerked off the hand and without glancing at the stranger began to jog away. It was a feeble effort and in no time the other feet were at par with her. She knew she needed the umbrella and if possible, those arms.

Sulli repeated the action again. This time she didn't hop away.

She had turned and sized him up. He was an amazingly well built athlete with markedly probing eyes. He did look younger than the beards he carried made him look and the right hand clutched the shaft of the umbrella as though to strangle it. She saw the thick veins decorating his dark hand and wished she could trace it beyond the rim of the red sweater he wore.

His voice too was striking- like a harmless knight, soft and soothing. It was possible God had seen her distress and sent her a dark angel.

'Compared to what,' she replied sorely. She paced up a little but always within the confines of his tent.

'Well, compared to another lady snugly fit in the arms of her man- somewhere.'

Though the words came from behind her ears, they flew right into her heart. This guy was an artist- making music out of her disappointment. She searched for the perfect response as they approached a rushing stream of fierce water.

In one crazy split second, he lifted her and hopped over with her. It was magical. She wished she could glue to his body.

'Thank you,'

She wasn't sure she had ever said a more sincere thank you in her life.

'It's okay,' Sulli smiled.

He had handed her the umbrella and then pulled off his sweaters to reveal a stunning chest- even though he still wore a t-shirt.

'Please wear for me. You are freezing.'

Aswa couldn't refuse. She was frozen and she also didn't want that chest hidden anymore.

That was the beginning of it all. They had ended the night on this particular bed.

Tonight, it was apparent another story was brewing. She was feeling de-ja vu.

'How much longer?' she asked flatly.

This woman was nuts. She knew him enough to know that whatever could make him keep sex at bay was no trifle matter. Women were just too lean-minded.

'Sleep and stop compounding my troubles.' It was a stern warning. He was her contract staff with United Nations currently on a just renewed six month contract. The lie wasn't too false. He was still a relief worker- only that he relieved highest bidders of their pests.

'What troubles?'

There was genuine concern in her voice but Sulli wanted none of that.

'Please sleep and stop being ridiculous.' It was an order.

Aswa wasn't going to be sheepish tonight.

'Did you just say ridiculous?' She shrugged off the duvet. 'Who has been acting all funny tonight? You or me?'

Sulli O'hib swallowed the question and once more reverted his attention to the last pages of the last book. In the scurried flip, Wee O'hib's photograph flew out and landed face up at the foot of the bed.

He stopped abruptly and bent over to retrieve it. He could feel a second frame.

It was so like his mother to keep caring even till now. He smiled broadly and separated Zwitt's picture from his mother's.

'Who are those?' Aswa probed, her saucer-sized eyes staring at both pictures. Sulli's relief was palpable enough to make her pry.

'My sweet mum.' He began. 'She is late though.' He separated both remarks with the anticipation of sympathy from Aswa. It was his hope too that she would ignore the second picture.

'Eh ya. Your mum is dead?' She felt really sorry for him. 'I am so sorry, baby.'

She crawled up to kiss his forehead and in the process earn a closer look at the pictures.

She took the pictures from him and studied the woman even more closely. The resemblance was unmistakeable.

Sulli held his breath and hoped she didn't dig further. He was suddenly hungry for food; all manners of food.

Aswa was not the one to stop halfway. She looked at the young boy in the picture.

'Was that you?'

Sulli nearly caught the bait but chose to let it pass. He wasn't going to be claiming a boy who would be dead soon. Besides his picture may make the rounds soon- post mortem.

'No that's not me.' He paused. 'A cousin. He used to live with my mum.'

The innocence on the boy's face was phenomenal. It didn't match Sulli's face. The boy looked strangely familiar but she could count on his right hand how many boys of that age he knew. She couldn't possibly know him.

She kissed Wee on the forehead too and smiled at the boy. She put the pictures aside and launched for Sulli's throat. Her tongue was thirsty for sweat.

Julie scrambled up from the floor and took her position. The queue had suddenly begun to move and despite the length of the wait, there was no sign of discontent. Everyone knew his slot-like it had been reserved from ancient times. She was unperturbed, memory-free and faceless.

Progression was slow and upwards as she marvelled at the beauty of the surroundings. She was clad in nothing- like everyone else and there were harmonious sounds oozing from unseen trumpets.

Alas it was her turn. It dawned on her that she was Julie- standing before supremacies outside the realm of reality.

Her records were shown in a flash and judgement passed. There were no words- just clips and tunes. Yet the communication was excellent.

As she found her way through the dazzlingly white vegetation and castles, there were only two residual names in her memory.

The first was Jehovah and for the sake of who she once was, the other was Zwitt.

14

Big time lawyer Joe Cupsay was not quite a big shot in bed. His marriage of four years was hanging by the slimmest thread.

They had improvised time without number And gone every length to teach him tricks that would satisfy his wife Christaine.

Currently, they were practising arousal using eccentric topics.

'If the fight had not been in the jungle,' he rhymed 'I assure you Mohammed Ali would have been downed.'

'No way,' she shouted. 'Am sure you don't know him.'

'Ali is the greatest. He will always be.'

Her hands kept at the main job. Trying to get him to perform this once.

It was a frustrating feeling. She was all ready.

But not he. He required loads and loads of ego massages and senseless talks.

The psychotherapist had recommended this last approach.

He opined that Joe always never left his work in the office.

The Physiotherapist had prescribed whole body exercises at night.

But pot-belly Joe never found the zeal to indulge.

Christaine would turn and twist while he sat and watched in despair.

Two years into their marriage, she had set up a task force.

Aimed to catch him. She was sure he was cheating.

But the task force had caught nobody and that incensed her the more.

There were no children- just both of them in an ebbing marriage.

She had gone the extra mile to solicit Lucy's advise.

After all it was his husband's job that plagued Joe's table.

The Empress had only reassured her more.

And armed herself with a vintage point.

'If Ali was invisible, Joe would not have knocked him off in the second fight.'

Christaine screamed. *At this point the only thing that is invisible is you.*

'I think there was so much at stake in that fight.' She countered. 'It was only fair he let him win. Don't forget he is a good muslim too.'

She retrieved her hand from the failed organ,

Cast him that knowing look that killed him the more.

'Christaine baby,'

'Please don't baby me,' she replied bluntly. She was more than fed up.

He went to shower. He had no idea whom to blame.

How could he tell her he had sustained erections for Lucy And even his latest secretary?

That one was an IED. He was not sure how long he was going to keep her.

At the pace they were going,

They would eventually get filmed or display to a gathering audience.

She was always turning him on. Gosh!

'Baby, Baby. Am on, am on.'

Christaine heard the chant and quickly ran into the bathroom.

It was like NEPA bringing light after three months of uninterrupted darkness.

Such enthusiasm and massive relief.

She indulged.

Lucy walked noiselessly into the office. She never had to pass through regular secretary protocol but at least, she usually knocked at Joe's entrance. She saw his head buried in the dailies and glided toward him.

'Hello Joww,' she greeted.

He was slightly surprised. He raised his glasses from the tilt that permitted him to read the tiny fonts on the newspaper.

'Common, you don't need specs to know it is me.' She snatched the glasses off his face.

'Lucy,' he grinned slightly. 'I know it is you.'

'Joww Joww,' she chanted 'how are you today?'

It appeared she came in peace today. Not a usual occurrence these days. They had been engaged in a recent contest for access to the Avri papers. He had maintained his ground and stood by his client.

He had done everything except informing Stephen of what domestic danger he bred.

'I am fine and you?' He curtly replied. He put his face to the newspaper. He knew that the longer he stared at Lucy, the more uncomfortable his zippers would become. He was neatly hidden under the desk but he just didn't want that.

Lucy called the bluff.

'We know you can't see jack without your glasses.'

He sniffed. 'Miracles do happen, Lucy.'

Lucy turned to face him. She rested faintly on the edge of the table and her heels rocked Joe's chair. He was a smallish man and in spite of his overtly big belly, his weight didn't seem to amount to much. He was as smart as he was brief. Lucy knew that from the onset and the chronic duels they had had buttressed that notion.

'Talking about miracles Joe,' she began. 'Are there more miracles in this office than usual?'

'I don't get you?'

'Of course you don't Joe.'

She got up and swayed to the curtains. The building tension in the room didn't deter Joe's eyes from following the bounce of her waist.

'Joe Cupsay, you will do exactly as I say henceforth or Christaine would become privy to the many miracles that Remi has been performing on you.'

He was shocked for a few seconds.

'You are a joker, Lucy.'

'You think so?'

She turned her gaze to the other end of the office. Joe followed her eyes. There was a transmitter neatly placed into the ceiling.

She saw his heart sink, smiled and galloped away. At the secretary's desk, she produced two bundles of a thousand naira note.

'You can now resign,' she instructed Remi.

Remi nodded and watched Madam walk away. She wished she could hold this measure of sway someday.

'Sit down,' Stephen shouted. 'Sit down.'

It was the quarterly meeting of the Avri Consolidated and the eight member board had been engaged in a fiery argument for over an hour.

Stephen had asked the Financial report to be read just minutes after the minutes of the last meeting was adopted.

Mr.Olusile had shifted uncomfortably on his chair and then started to flip through his files. It appeared he had not expected the request. Stephen was bemused at first but two minutes later and Olusile was still fumbling.

'What is this Mr.Olusile?'

'Excuse me,' It was Bowono who spoke up. He had patiently waited for Stephen to notice Olusile's unpreparedness before he could intervene. His script was timed to perfection. On the other hand, Olusile had no idea how it was going to happen. He had been informed a fortnight ago not to worry about preparing any financial reports at the next meeting. So he had simply been caught off-guard by Stephen's request. His informant, Dere sat just opposite him.

'Yes.'

Stephen motioned Bow to speak.

'I find it rather puzzling that we should be demanding about financial reports when we know full well that things have taken a downward spiral at Avri's.'

'Yes. Things have taken spirals- downwards or upwards, only figures can confirm,' Stephen interjected.

'Stephen, allow me to finish.'

Stephen backed down. There was some growing air of majesty around Bowono. Even the other board members seemed to recognise it.

'My point is this,' Bow continued. 'In the recent past, our CEO has taken unsolicited liberty in making wanton investments.'

Stephen thundered. 'Bow, you are not serious.'

'Allow me to make my point, Stephen Avri.'

Again, surprisingly he let him.

'By this time last year, we had grown almost seven percent of our projected ten percent rise for the year.'

He glanced across the room. 'My friends, this is the final quarter of the year and all pointers show that we had not only refused to grow- we have somersaulted from the leading conglomerate in West Africa to a groping neck-deep in debt one man show.' He took in his audience.

'I am in a privileged position to tell you that we have not only invested foolishly, we have invested blindly in the past seven months.'

The room was pin silent. Stephen noted some nodding heads. He wondered where Bow bought the courage to address him like a paid labourer in his own company. Their relationship had been mechanical in recent weeks- or months. So mechanical that he eased him off his mind. He couldn't remember the last time they shared any joke but that was because he was busy. As he listened to Bow's oration, he felt the room get smaller and smaller. All eyes were undoubtedly on him as they anticipated his trademark counter rage and defence of company policy.

He wished he still had that fire.

'I think it is only appropriate to ask Stephen what happened to the twenty seven million dollars we earmarked for investments in the Saudi economy.'

All eyes turned to him again.

'Are you done?' he asked rather too calmly for a man on the hot seat.

'I am not,' Bowono replied. 'I think we should equally ask him what happened to our Deputy CEO- Julie.'

Everyone saw the blood rush into Stephen's face. That was a below the belt punch from Bow.

'Sit down!' He screamed and raged persistently.

Bow didn't reply him. He made sure he stood for as long as he wanted before he sat down.

Stephen was wounded. He packed his brief case and left the meeting.

'My friends,' Bow addressed the remaining six people. 'Truth hurts, they say yet we must not shy away from it.'

Majority nodded.

'The events of today will show you at least one thing. That Stephen is not emotionally stable to head this consortium.'

'Yes he is not,' Dere re-echoed.

'We cannot abandon our hopes and dreams to the dictates of an emotionally labile man.'

He stopped just short of calling him mad. I think we are safer if we place him on suspension until he sorts himself out.

The idea was well received. They did a quick vote and only Joe Cupsay's hand believed Stephen should be retained. Every other person voted for Bowono Jereny as the interim Head of the Consortium. The margins were wide and Bow got up to thank everyone for the trust and responsibility assigned to him. He had noted Joe's vote but Lucy had assured him she had him shadowed.

It was a good day at the office-after all.

Stephen sat at the front pew of the empty church and reminisced on the vanity of life.

To Err is Woman

He had not come this close to the altar in many years and even today, he felt some form of peace just sitting and staring at the slain Saviour. He had been an altar-boy at thirteen- but somewhere along the ladder, he had shifted focus.

Self-actualisation had usurped the place of religious fanaticism and he had vigorously pursued the former. He had no regrets. He did achieve many of his dreams. The only hitch was the dream that culminated in Julie's death. He identified that moment as the sour point of his epic life. He had made good success until the knife betrayed him and then henceforth, it had been betrayals all the way.

He adjusted himself on the hard seat and rolled away the urge to get on his knees and pray.

Pray about what. He had no needs. He was becoming a little numb to the events that defined life. He was sure he had lived a good life up till now.

His phone rang again. He just endured the distraction. His battery life would soon finish and everyone would rest.

It was Joe calling him again.

He decided to pick.

'Stephen where are you?'

'In my father's house,'

'Stephen, listen to me. Wherever you are, you are not quite safe.'

Stephen listened.

'Did you get my sms?'

'Haven't read it.'

'Listen to me,' he repeated. 'You need to trust me on this. I sent you a message earlier. The police have issued a warrant for your arrest and it's the same old case.'

No response. He continued. 'They say there is overwhelming evidence that you murdered Julie.'

Stephen heaved.

'At the same time,' Joe paused. He was not sure this man could take all the hard blows in this state. He changed his mind. The sinister tale of the takeover of the company by Lucy and the subsequent court injunction restricting him from coming close to this firm could wait. At least till they met.

'At the same time, you know we have been through a lot together. I know you cannot harm a fly- not to talk of Julie.'

How did he come to that conclusion. The people that ought to know were the ones stabbing him in the face.

'We have come a long way Av,' Joe reassured him. 'This is not the time to turn around and disappear.'

'I have not disappeared,' Stephen negated. 'At least you could still reach me. You just told me i am a wanted man.'

'True, the authorities have demanded for your immediate arrest but we cant solve that on the phone.'

Joe glanced around his wound up car and searched for transmitters- A once bitten man's approach.

'I have a private apartment off Ibeju, kinda remote underdeveloped area but it can steal you away for as long as you intend to stay underground.'

He was listening.

'Let me know where you are so I can come pick you.' He searched for more persuasive words. 'We can use the time to prepare a defense.'

'Joe,' Stephen began.

The phone beeped twice in his ears and went blank.

His battery had finally betrayed him too.

He dropped the phone beside him and trotted within the church. It was amazing how holy churches become on Sundays and today, it was almost like an abandoned museum with its high roof and traditional celestial decorations.

The baptism podium had an inscription on it. *Come unto me all ye that thirst and i will give you rest.*

He opened the vault that contained the baptismal water. It contained some quantity of clean water.

He thirsted. He really did. He bent over and sucked from the bowl. It was refreshing and then it was tasty.

He stopped when his throat seemed not to hurt anymore.

Then he turned left and entered the confession box. He hoped he could find some rest as he shut the door and slumped on the floor.

He sincerely prayed to find rest.

As Sulli reclined on the Sofa in Neho's office, he felt he had over prepared for this mission. He had his gun on his waist and a small dagger strapped to the holster on the other side of the waist. Those were emergency measures but it didn't seem likely that he would need any.

The conversation with Neho had started crudely as anticipated but they had instantly warmed up the moment he tendered his identity card- fifty thousand naira. He had obtained them in minty fifty naira notes and he saw the glee in her eyes when the money changed sides.

'What exactly do you want?'

Sulli smiled. He was not the only one under this magical money spell.

'I want to see my little nephew Zwitt.'

'Oh..Zwitt the darling,' she whimped.

She obviously had not paid any attention to all Sulli had said in the earlier ten minutes.

'That boy is one of the nicest we have got.' She eyed Sulli. 'And I can see why.'

She really could see why. This stranger had just changed the fortunes of her weekend. She had spent the previous night wondering on what excuses would perfectly rule her out from being a part of Mrs.Tunji's aso-ebi train. She couldn't afford the lace they imposed on the committee of friends and she didn't have the boldness to state so. All of a sudden, her miracle had come.

She was excited, eager to help. Fifty thousand naira would go a long way but she was optimistic that if she co-operated, she may have another bundle for the road.

She sprang up in her most energetic fashion. She opened the register and stared curiously into it, reciting the names aloud.

'Bende Chuma...no...Jackson Iwu...no....Zwitt Avri...that's it.'

He was almost screaming.

'Ok Mister Avri,' she put the Avri badge on Sulli. 'I will go get him straight away.'

She started to hum. 'Cubicle D, Room 6.' Her memory needed that.

A little above five minutes later, they were back.

'Common Zwitt,' Neho cajoled from behind him. 'Go say hi to your uncle.'

Zwitt had instantly frozen at the door. Her arms were on his shoulder and she was almost shoving him in.

There was no traces of recognition on Zwitt's face. She could not see that because she led from behind.

'Very shy boy. You should know.'

Sulli nodded briskly sitting up to study his target.

'But once he settles in, he is a charmer.' Neho continued.

'Hello Zwitt.'

The boy stared at him- unmoved but pensive.

Zwitt liked the voice. He had been annoyed to be hassled up from sleep to come see his uncle. He had bluntly told Mrs Neho he had no uncles but she wouldn't hear. Fifty thousand naira could never lie. When he stopped in his tracks at the door, he took the time to assess who had come for him. He was a total stranger but he didn't look quite dangerous. He had this volatile smile that he hadn't seen in months. He had felt the matron pushing him from behind and then decided to proceed.

The man wore a mickey mouse tee-shirt within a grey jacket. Zwitt loved Mickey and as he walked towards Sulli, his eyes were fixed on the Mickey in his chest.

Sulli sustained the fake smile for as long as he could. He didn't like the trance-like steps the boy was taking and the way he stared at his heart. He felt a burning sensation on his heart. It had never been there- it was not a light burn. It hurt like a piercing hot blade repeatedly going through his heart. He stretched forth his right hands to welcome his nephew- the latter didn't reciprocate. He just kept coming in those measured steps- almost oblivious of his presence and his eyes stuck to his chest.

Sulli was sweating by the time Zwitt reached him. Then the hurt on the chest stopped as he sat him on his laps.

Neho wasn't watching. She had no time for more melodramatic scenes; the assorted rats here gave her more than enough. She stared at the long list of names on her register and wished someone would just come with a truck and carry many of them away- Of course in exchange for some hard currency. These boys were turning into men on his head and with the way most of them were going, they would leave the orphanage for the prison. She searched her book of tricks for another means to milk this Uncle.

'So Mr.Avri,' she started. 'What are your plans?'

Sulli looked up.

'At the moment, nothing.' Neho's face fell.

He continued. 'I recently came into town and i heard that he was here so i decided to come see him.' He paused. 'We have not seen since he was two.'

Neho wasn't interested.

'I will have to work out the modalities for his exit from your facility.'

Modalities. That was the word Neho needed to hear. She swallowed hard.

'That sounds fine. You can take him for a short stroll within the compound. Everyone needs to bond.' She was chuckling.

Sulli put the boy down and got up. 'That's so kind of you. I am most impressed at your disposition.'

Neho waved him not to worry and then watched them exit the office.

A few steps away from Neho's office, Zwitt yanked his hands off Sulli's grip.

'I know you are not my Uncle anything.' He turned to face him, twisting his neck backwards and uncomfortably. 'I know you are not my Uncle,' he repeated.

Sulli didn't like it when he looked at him. The chest was starting to hurt again.

'Of course i am your Uncle,' he replied.

'No, you are not.' The boy was obstinate.

Zwitt grabbed his hands again. 'But i will pretend like you are.' They walked a yard more. 'Just because i like you.'

Sulli had no suitable response. The boy was stealing his show. It was obvious he had powers that he didn't come prepared for. He allowed Zwitt lead him to the playground.

It was as if they had switched roles- and Zwitt was the elder of the both.

'I will show you my friends and better pray- they like you too or you are in deep soup.'

Sulli smiled. He was already in deep soup. He liked the boy. Seemed to remind him of the innocent latently stubborn boy he once was.

But there was money to be made. He didn't want to end his career on a disappointing low.

He tagged along. 'They would like me.'

Parents listen to your children..we are the leaders of tomorrow...
Geria hid inside the big chest in the principal's office and listened to the proceedings of the end of week after school assembly. It was usually a rowdy one, the palpable excitements from the kids who their parents may have made numerous promises to usually, drowned the voice of their teachers. Nevertheless, there were routine recitals and admonishments to the little ones. Everyone played final pranks, behaving only when a

teacher's eyes were visibly fixed on him. Even the teachers looked forward to this tradition. Fresh air was panacea.

There was no reason to go home, Geria had concluded. Last weekend was more hell than the one before it. Everything was on a downward spiral and she missed Zwitt terribly.

As the final beg rang for classes to close, she wondered where she could find space enough to hide. There was no way she would return home this weekend. Her little mind was determined and just as her pencil entered her school bag, she had the answer.

As other feet darted to the assembly ground, she made a smart sidestep and briskly walked to the big chest she had pictured moments earlier. She was lucky it was unlocked so she carefully crouched beside the many books and closed the door after her. The minty smell of the books nauseated her initially. She was sure her French textbook would be in here but there was not enough space to turn her neck. The same French textbook that she had received a slap from Lucy for demanding she bought her a copy.

'Until you become reasonable,' her mother had sneered at her.

She sniffed. When things eased up, she could read the whole book overnight. French was her favourite subject.

Lucy parked facing the school gate bars and watched the erratic display on the assembly ground. She was not quite impressed with the level of discipline she saw. That is how it starts, she told herself. If little children could not maintain absolute silence before their teachers on the assembly ground, there was no sacred ground. In her days, no one dared to move without instruction. All the muscles but the ears were put on inert mode. In her days, there was fear for elders- teachers and mothers.

She glanced around a second time. She hadn't spotted her little rebel yet. George was conspicuous as ever. She had seen him throwing red dust to the winds and laughing as his mates ran and cursed. Most of the entire dust settled on him; he didn't run with them but had stood laughing like a moron. Lucy sighed and searched the third time for her daughter. In spite of her stubbornness, she had more hope in her than this budding testosterone-George. She had an opinion, and the will to follow her opinions through. All Lucy needed to do was tame her a little. Teach her hierarchy and respect for her mother.

'Where is your sister?'

George had shown up alone.

'I don't know.'

He was not interested even. He opened the front door and entered. Lucy was slightly worried. She alighted from the car and walked several yards into the school compound.

Just then it stuck her.

Her little rascal could probably be hiding behind any of the shrubs and feasting on the confusion she was about to trigger.

She spurned around. She wasn't going to give a four year old that satisfaction of fooling her.

In the car, she kept tapping on the steering and counting down. Her eyes still searched the nearest hide-outs.

'You mean you didn't see her at all?'

George was already drowsy. He just shook his head and wished his mother didn't disturb him again.

Three minutes after counting down from two hundred, Lucy brought the engine to life and drove off. She was sure a disappointed Geria would soon surrender herself to the school authorities. They would probably ring her before she got home.

She glanced at her phone every other minute.

Geria opened her sleepy eyes to the faint sound coming from outside the chest. She held her breath and listened. The tiny slit between the doors of the closet had been obliterated and she could hear the feet leaving the office- shutting windows and turning off sockets. It was apparently the security man doing his final rounds. She pushed the door to the closet. It didn't move an inch.

Suddenly it dawned on her that the chest had been padlocked. She was sweating already and had actually woken up to the diminished oxygen supply in her cage.

She banged her feeble hands on the door and screamed.

'Zwitt,'

She continued to call him until her last energy sipped away. There was no point calling another. He was the only one who stood by her in years gone by.

She closed her eyes to the hurt on her chest. When she woke up, she was sure the door would be open and she could read her French all night.

Tears flowed like never before. This time, real tears from a heart in utter anguish. Reality was even made more hurting by the events that ushered it in.

She tried to push away the memories, to distract herself repeatedly but they were futile.

It was Saturday late evening and she had just dropped Geria's body at the morgue- accompanied by a stunned Bowono. There were no explanations for the unexpected decay that had culminated in the death.

It kept playing in her head. How she could have averted everything if she had only been a mother at that defining hour. She had carried George home and resumed her Friday afternoon chores- precisely as planned. She drove the over two kilometres traffic-heavy distance to her lawyer. He had asked her to present the last of the evidences as they finalised their case against Stephen. The meeting didn't last too long. She was distracted-

especially by the fact that no one had called to report Geria's turn-up. Instead, there were calls from her new squad at the office and complaints from some of the people she had laid off just that Friday. She was instituting a new order and as such she had to field her loyalists.

As the uneasiness grew, she excused herself and drove home. On the way, she knew it was almost impossible for Geria to have been returned home. Their gate had a password and she doubted if Geria knew the permutations. Anything was possible with that smart mind.

She entered the sitting room at exactly eight minutes past seven. George was up and staring listlessly at the television. It was his hitherto favourite cartoon- Ben 10 but today, he looked too lonely to enjoy the heroics. The window blinds were parted just above the seat he sat. He had apparently been staring out in search of a companion. Lucy had smiled- understanding the intense loneliness the young boy was subjected to. It was strange that this was the same house that burst with life less than a year ago.

'Hello G,' she announced her presence.

'Hello Mum,' he responded. Then he reluctantly got up to embrace her. Even that act was unusual- not while Ben 10 was on the set.

Lucy held him close to her chest.

'Dont worry,' she whispered. 'Soon, mummy will make you plenty little ones to play with.'

George nodded and stuck to her chest.

Lucy disengaged and quickly glanced across the room.

'Geria home yet?'

He shook his head.

This was not good at all. Lucy walked to her bedroom and began to make calls.

It was all her fault. The torrential tears came again. She played the story back and front. The real story depicted a terrible mother. The world didn't need to hear that story. Everyone would curse and nail her and she didn't need that now. She needed sympathy more than any other thing.

She had started her deception with the call to Bowono. Even at that point, she was not anticipating the eventual outcome but her instincts led her right.

'Bow, Geria has not showed up all afternoon. She told me earlier she would visit her friend Queen.'

There was minimal fright in her voice.

'Have you called Queen's mom?'

That was a lapse. She hesitated briefly.

'Her number isn't connecting,' she lied.

'This is what we do,' Bow instructed. 'You call her for another thirty minutes and if there's still no success, you let me know.'

Lucy nodded into the phone. Thirty minutes seemed like forever at this point.

'I will drop by at their house on my way home.'

'Ok. That's fine.'

It was one good aspect out of many. Bow knew how to take her cross personal.

Meanwhile she went ahead to tighten the loose nut. Of course neither Queen nor her mother had seen Geria. Queen saw her last at the end of classes that day.

She had ordered a sullen George into the car as her mind fired in every direction. Stephen was still at large. It was possible he had abducted the little girl to get back at her.

She had rung up her police friend to intimate him of the development- suggesting they double efforts to bring Stephen in. She had no other enemy she could think of at this time. As she sped towards the school, she called the School Headmistress who tried to calm her down. She promised to call up the relevant teachers and get as many hands as she could down to the school that night.

In retrospect, it appeared that Geria was death bound. Otherwise why had the school's recently acquired generator refused to come on after electricity had gone off five minutes into their search. They resorted to phone torches and security torches. The young teachers were sure Geria would be fine and safe- hopefully in another pupil's home. It was an assurance that Lucy found stupid- considering the fact that the headmistress had in her presence called all the parents' phone numbers on her log book. They had no idea. Infact, it spread more panic across.

Lucy braved up and dialled Stephen's number. She hadn't done that in weeks. The number was switched off. It gave more credence to her theory.

Stephen was playing with red hot charcoal, she mused.

Infact, it was she that called the search off for the night.

'I know it is him,' she had said on a final note to Bow. The latter had also come to the school to assist in any way possible. 'He feels he can get away with this?'

Bow had just shook his head. 'He is actually building up more cases against himself.'

'Of course, another count of kidnapping won't be bad.' She was ecstatic. 'It even lends credence to the allusion of insanity.'

She blew her nose into her very wet scarf. How was she going to live the rest of her life with that image of a crouched up Geria in rigor mortis. Eyes shut as though she slept in peace. The stench from her uniform was remarkable. Infact it was the stench of ammonia and then the drying stream of urine from the closet that had drawn the attention of the office cleaner on Saturday morning.

She- not being privy to the search of the earlier night had gone ahead to open the locker.

The rest was history.

Lucy was there in less than thirty minutes. She had arrived unexpectant as the headmistress had just called to say they had found Geria. She walked through the soft barricade of teachers- her heart pounded as she wondered on what reaction was most appropriate for a stubborn little girl. She didn't bother to observe the faces of the women and read off the shock in their eyes. The headmistress however made a failed attempt to intimate her but in her arrogant style, she waved her away. She didn't need no child-training lectures from no education certificate holder. In the corners of her mind, she was not very happy Geria was found this soon. She would have loved if a police raid of Stephen had yielded her amongst other results. She had already slated a brief press conference for eleven in the morning.

At precisely three minutes past nine, she met the rudest shock of her life. Her daughter had been left as she had been found inside the closet.

It was a terrible sight. She had passed out almost immediately. It had never crossed her mind that this was it.

'Geria, Geria,' she murmured into the pillow. No position seemed to assuage her distress. She had no idea where George was. She thought she had at some point given the headmistress permission to keep him with her family until things eased up.

Bowono had tried all day to console her. This was way beyond him. He too had given her a break. She stared around the empty room. Threr were only echoes and flashes of that moment. She needed answers. It was possible someone assaulted Geria sexually and dumped her there. It was possible she hid out of fear from an abductor. She wondered what had been in her final thoughts as she gasped for air. She had demanded for an investigation and an autopsy. She was going to give her last blood to see that justice was done with her beloved daughter.

Just then, the owl cried.

Otima waved his penis for the final time. He could not understand why his urine had recently begun to come in inconsistent droplets. He was pressed, he strained and made grunts in a bid to muster more energy. Another drop fell from the tip of his penis.

He shook his head in painful realisation. His enemies were winning this battle. This particular blow was a very cruel one. He was never going to come so low to the point of telling any other man the funny games his private part now played. Even telling his wife was still under deliberation.

He fastened his trousers and headed back into the house- the urge to urinate was still there.

So also was the urge to revenge. Just last week, he had eventually obtained the little calabash from Aguiwu- the renowned revengist and diabolicist. It was not any complicated. He had gone very prepared- financially and with material-wise. The little evil man had asked him repeatedly what he wanted.

'I want him dead,' Otima stated each time.

The man would then draw lines on the floor with his white chalk. Otima noticed he only saw the white lines at the point he drew them. Then they vanished or melted. The physics of that didn't appeal to him. He had watched the man carefully- hoping in his heart that this would be his final Juju-stop.

'Open your hands.'

He did. Aguiwu cupped his own hands and then opened it inside Otima's. His hands were swallowed in the latter's palms but when he withdrew, Otima had in his hands a tiny pot- the size of a regular tomato.

'Shake it,' he instructed.

Otima did.

'That is his life.' He paused.

Otima followed his eyes across the dim shrine. There were fresh preparation of sacrifices just behind him and blood trickled from an animal head to the floor. He appeared to be looking for something or listening to something.

'Everytime you shake it, he experiences turmoil.'

Otima shook it again.

'I have given you the rare option of making him suffer before he dies.'

'Thank you so much, Aguiwu the great one.'

'You have his whole life in your hands.' He stood up. 'You can vent as your heart wishes.'

The last words came from the inside chambers.

Otima had secured his prize against his wrapper and literally ran home. He was hopeful the water in the pot experienced a measure of upheavals as he negotiated the bends through the forest. He returned a very relieved man.

Even Enema had noticed the change. He could not share his discovery with her since he had promised her to leave vengeance to God.

He still considered that option; only that plan B gave him a deserved edge. In any case, he had hidden his magic inside the saddle of his abandoned bicycle. There was really no other place he could think of as safe. Enema's extensive reach and intuitive abilities always uncovered anything he tried to hide. He had laced this one on the insides of the saddle as though it mattered little and it had stayed inert until the second day of his dysuria.

The pain had struck his back so bad that instead of urine streams, tears had poured out from his eyes. That was just five days after he returned from Aguiwu. His enemy was stepping up the game and he could not afford to let the sleeping pot lie.

That night, he had tiptoed from the bed to the bicycle and given the pot a violent shake. He could hear the splash of the fluid against the container. It was at that point that he first thought of feed-backs. In the real sense, he was only trusting this tiny man. There was no gauge to assess the impact of the shakes on Stephen. He hoped he had shaken him enough to deter further assaults on his penis.

Tonight, it was just obvious he needed to do more. He had a burden on his head and a new one on his waist. It hurt him even as he walked back to the bed.

'You are not happy.'

She had seen through the darkness- as usual.

Otima cleared his throat. 'How can I be happy when our daughter is lying in some mortuary so far away.'

Enema put her arm on his chest.

He continued, 'When her killer is going about free and unapologetic.'

'My husband, worry will not take us far from grief.' She began her counselling session.

Otima listened for a short while but the peppery sensation on his groin couldn't let him concentrate.

Stephen was winning this battle and yet he had the joker. When was he going to use it? After the idiot had killed him?

He gently put away Enema's hands.

'My dear, worry will not take us anywhere o.'

He stood up. He had something that would take them somewhere. He left an unsuspecting Enema on the bed again and calmly walked to his bicycle- taking the pain in his strides.

He did not waste any time.

He uncovered the tiny pot and shook it with all of his might. Then he smashed it against the wall. The water splattered some distance from the wall even unto him.

'You will go first,' he muttered into the air.

The owl cried.

Stephen got up and descended from the pulpit. In over three nights of lodging in the hospital, he had desecrated almost every part. Yesternight, he had slept behind the altar veils with the angels. They didn't seem to notice him and he reciprocated the gesture and stuck to his business- sleep and stints of worry in between.

During the day, he sat from one pew to another. He was especially lucky that the church was rather poorly patronized during the week and the few faithful that came never returned.

Sunday was going to be different. He needed to find an alternative- perhaps endless rest.

It was pretty dark outside. The lampposts showed yellow lights that found the darkness near impenetrable. He had parked his car at the mechanics and now he felt for the keys in his pockets. They weren't there. The last time he recalled seeing them was yesterday night behind the veils. It was not like he needed them. The car made him conspicuous and traceable. The only downside was that he couldn't now visit his house.

There were places he could go. He only had to keep moving- away from suspecting eyes and the police cuffs.

Bigard Street was its usual self. He had been walking for about an hour, jostling in between packed vehicles when he was on the main road. Surrounded now by a swarm of entropic people, he felt more relaxed. His steps were tailored and he avoided every form of eye contact. He hadn't eaten anything reasonable these past days- just snacks and drinks from the shops beside the church.

He wasn't hungry though. His only desire was to keep moving. That had pretty much been his motto in life. *Keep moving.* He stumbled into empty cans of drinks repeatedly and made enough noise to make heads turn briefly. He noticed he wasn't lifted his feet as high as he ought to while he walked. But he couldn't help it. He moved on. He would eventually find rest somewhere.

People were starting to stretch out on the bodies of car parked beside houses- sleeping positions apparently. He was the latest entry to the league of homeless people- at least for one day and he would probably return to the church or never.

He saw a red E-class outside one of the houses just off Bigard Street. The street was less densely loafed and that made it a bad spot for him to crash. He owned one such car- Julie's own he recalled. He approached the car by default, his eyes lighting up with quick memories.

Then he saw a familiar sticker- *DON'T TALK WHEN I'M SMILING.* It was certainly hers.

He studied the building closer.

He was not sure which street he was but there were chances it was Bowono's house.

He pushed his hand through the slit on the gate and undid the bolt from inside. He was a fugitive. He could also play detective.

The front door was locked and the lights off. He poked at the window nearest to the door. It was hinged on the inside. He dutifully checked each of the windows till he found an open one. There was no way he could get in without support from inside. He needed a lift from outside to be able to bend under the lifted frame and enter noiselessly.

There were voices in his head, directing him in his local dialect. They showed him where a stool was and he brought it.

He stood on the shaky stool and masterfully glided into the apartment. Right leg first, then left and his whole body was in. The darkness gave him an advantage. He had heard Lucy's voice from outside and it was the glee that incensed him more.

Bow's more serious voice came in occasional spurts. Stephen could not follow their conversation from where he stood. He traced Lucy's voice, by passed the bedroom. The local voices in his head asked him to peep. He stared instead. The sheets were scattered on the floor. He could see her pink pants- she always did pink- and her brassiere on the side table. Her shoes had nearly fallen him when he was in the parlor. There was a male boxer on the floor too. Stephen's palm was moist. His throat dried up and he felt some strange hunger pangs.

'O Bow, i really could not have...' The voice tailed off. He completed it in his head.

'Dont worry Baby, i always got you here.'

Bow's deeply romantic voice reminded him again that there was another man in the house.

They were in the shower, enjoying each other's presence as much as the sprinkles from the shower.

Stephen studied them from his vintage position for a while.

She was a seductive figure especially in nudity. He wondered if this was all the driving force Bow needed to become Chief antagonist. It was not his fault. The local voices took over proceedings again.

They had destroyed his life with their schemes. The least he could do was become who they insisted he was.

He had to hurry, the voices reminded him. He needed rest. He pranced away from the bathroom into the kitchen. Thankfully Bow's cutlery were displayed in neat sequence. He made his selection. A smaller knife for Lucy and then a butcher's knife for Bow. He was skilled with knives. He had done it before.

'You know I am not going to wait for you to finish?' Bow declared.

It was not their first time.

'There you go again,' Lucy replied. 'Always inpatient even in romance.'

It confirmed his thoughts. They had been at this for some while and he never knew.

He back tracked and was only saved the embarrassment of being caught in no man's land by Lucy's call out to Bow.

'Bow nah. How can you leave with the towel?' Then she added, 'You just never learn.'

Bow returned to sublet the towel to her and in those few seconds, Stephen found a perfect spot behind the door to the bedroom.

A refreshed Bow stepped in, dangling his exhausted penis and rubbing his hands to fend off the cold from the Aircondition.

Just beyond the door, he stopped. Stephen wasn't in any way anxious. There were no permutations to his mission tonight.

Only one outcome was possible- somebody's dying and in the interim, he had the element of surprise and the weapon.

He could see the goose bumps on Bow's body but he chose not to strike. He knew instinctually that he would always go to the mirror next. He was a vain guy and those moments of self awareness helped his ego. Stephen made his choice.

He wanted to see the split panic on his face from the reflections in the mirror before he plunged.

Lucy just began the real bathing so he had at least five minutes to finish this up.

Bow moved on- to size himself in the mirror.

Stephen dropped both knives and with his toes drew a screw driver closer to himself. He didn't want to make many cuts on this glorious body. It was bad enough that he was going to die naked.

Bow was starting to put some facial cream on. That meant his eyes were closing and opening in between rubs.

Stephen struck. A clean wide angled swipe at the root of his neck- just where the artery of life showed its fragile head-was all it took.

The helpless surprise on Bow's face made sure he couldn't scream. He only had the liberty of seeing who downed him from the reflections on the mirror.

There were no final words for his friend.

Stephen pulled out the six inches screw driver and the blood splashed and then started to gush. It caught his wrist a little but it mattered not at all.

He sidestepped as Bow eventually fell face down on the floor.

He wished he had more time, he would have given him a lesson on loyalty- just in case he were to re-incarnate. He left the body there and picked up his knives.

He reasoned that he didn't need both of them. He was not sure if the greater or lesser evil lay ahead.

Lucy had a chance of being difficult and elusive. He was not sure how he wanted to finish her but he walked triumphantly to the bathroom- closing the bedroom door after his exit.

He met her in good condition- drying her hair with the ends of the towel.

She was even prettier than he remembered her. There was that stint in her eyes. Stephen knew it was her hallmark of sexual satisfaction.

It all happened too fast.

Lucy saw Stephen, the towel dropped from her hands and before she could say anything, he had given his first slash.

It caught her on her left breast taking the nipple and some fat with her.

Before the nipple could touch ground, he had swiped again. This time he hacked into her back as she tried to dodge the trajectory.

Her screams sounded like music to his ears. She had fallen over the toilet seat, hitting her head against the sink but the zeal to live kept her conscious but drowsy.

Stephen settled leg astride over her and began to piece away her life in mad fury.

'This is for all the pain you caused me,' he kept repeating as blood and pieces of flesh followed each stab.

When he was tired, he could hear the voice again urging him to find rest.

He glanced remorselessly across the bathroom. He wished he didn't have to stain the white tiles with such filthy blood.

He got up and returned to the bedroom.

The voice ordered him to lie down.

He couldn't resist any more. He created some place on the other side of the floor, beside the bed and laid down.

It was that kind of day, that kind of life and now he was very ready to face any charges for his misgivings.

Native words	Translation
Akamu	processed maize flour
Uno-ekwu	traditional kitchen- often a small hut by the corner of the main house
Agbada	overflowing gown
Unere	plantain
Oghe-agu	Local market
Ha jukwia taa, ha elie ya echi	If they refuse it today, they will eat it tomorrow
O te aka odiwalu njo, odi mma	Things always get better with time